AF283624

IMAGES
of England

THE ARUN
NAVIGATION

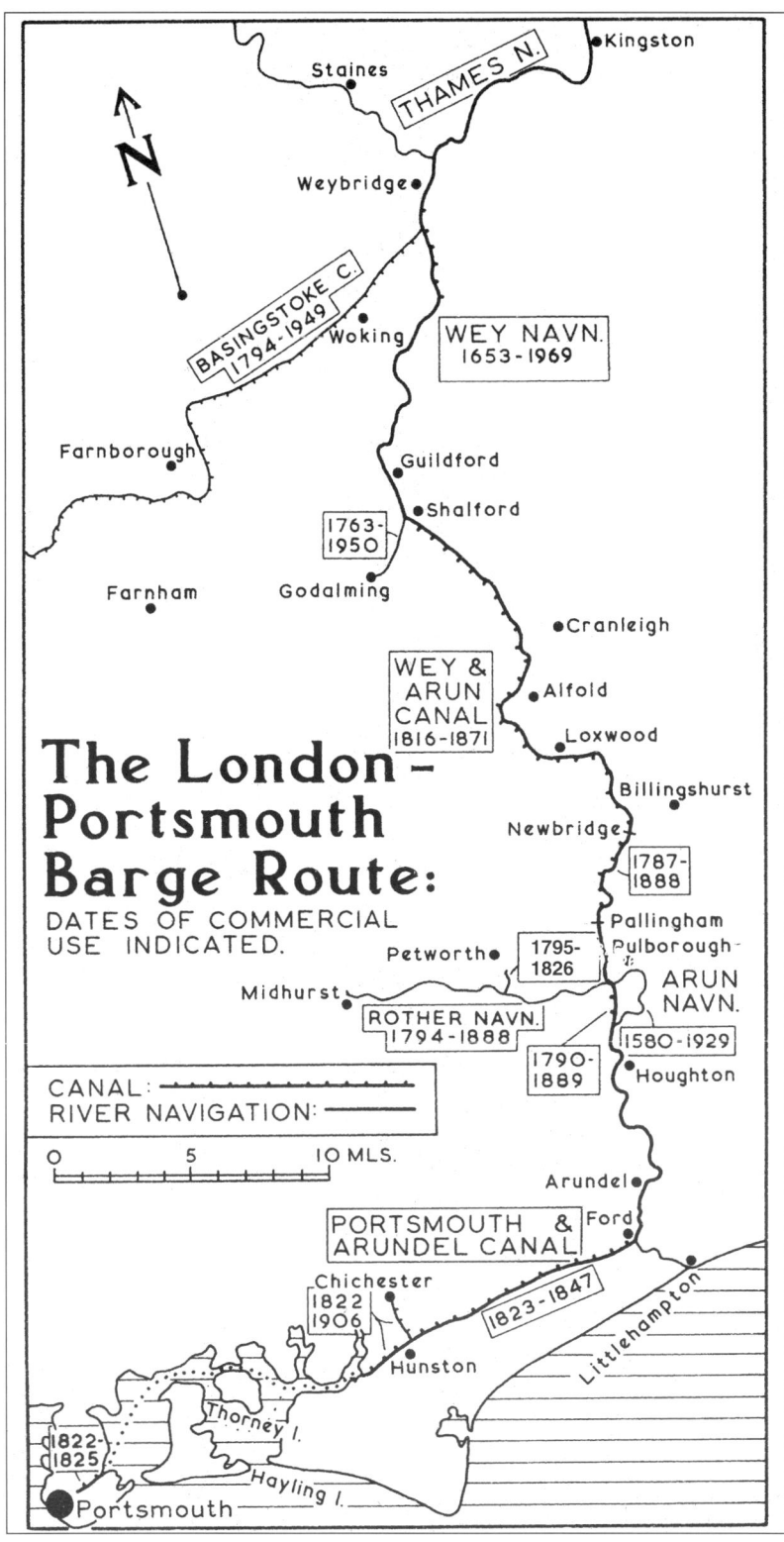

The London-Portsmouth Barge Route: map showing dates of commercial use indicated.

Kingston • Staines • THAMES N. • Weybridge •

N

BASINGSTOKE C. 1794-1949 • Woking •

WEY NAVN. 1653-1969

Farnborough •

Guildford • Shalford •

1763-1950 • Godalming •

Farnham •

Cranleigh •

WEY & ARUN CANAL 1816-1871 • Alfold • Loxwood •

Billingshurst •

Newbridge •

1787-1888

The London-Portsmouth Barge Route:
DATES OF COMMERCIAL USE INDICATED.

Petworth • 1795-1826 • Pallingham • Pulborough

Midhurst •

ROTHER NAVN. 1794-1888

ARUN NAVN.

1790-1889 • 1580-1929 • Houghton •

CANAL: ————
RIVER NAVIGATION: ——

0   5   10 MLS.

Arundel •

PORTSMOUTH & ARUNDEL CANAL • Ford

Chichester • 1822 1906 • 1823-1847 • Littlehampton

Hunston •

Thorney I.

1822-1825 • Hayling I.

• Portsmouth

IMAGES
of England

THE ARUN
NAVIGATION

P.A.L. Vine

TEMPUS

First published 2000
Copyright © P.A.L. Vine, 2000

Tempus Publishing Limited
The Mill, Brimscombe Port,
Stroud, Gloucestershire, GL5 2QG

ISBN 0 7524 2103 4

Typesetting and origination by
Tempus Publishing Limited
Printed in Great Britain by
Midway Clark Printing, Wiltshire

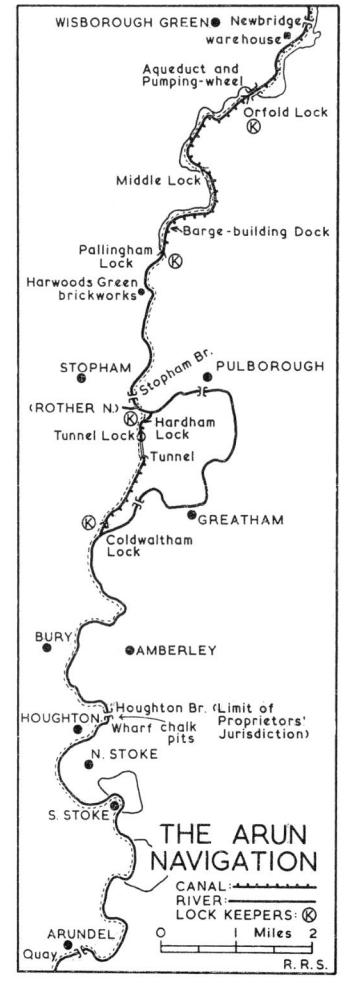

Contents

ANNO SEXTO

GEORGII II. REGIS.

****

C A P. XII.

An Act for erecting Piers in and for repairing and keeping in repair the Harbour of *Little Hampton*, called *Arundel Port*, in the County of *Sussex*.

WHEREAS it is a great Encouragement to Trade and Navigation to have good Harbours and Ports for receiving of Shipping: And whereas the Harbour of *Little Hampton*, called *Arundel Port*, in the County of *Sussex*, was heretofore a safe Harbour, and capable of receiving Ships and Vessels of a considerable Burthen, but a Beach being now thrown up by the Sea the said Harbour is thereby become choked up, and the Navigation of the River *Arun*, commonly called *Arundel River*, obstructed, and the said Harbour rendered almost useless, to the great Damage of the Inhabitants of the said Town of *Arundel*: And whereas the said Harbour cannot be restored, improved, and preserved, unless a Channel be cut through the said Beach and Piers, and Locks erected and made in proper Places: And whereas the Inhabitants of the said Town are unable to raise a sufficient Sum of Money to defray the Expence of carrying on, completing, and preserving so useful and beneficial an Undertaking, without the Aid and Assistance of Parliament: May it therefore please Your Majesty that it may be enacted; and be it enacted by the King's most Excellent Majesty, by and with the Advice and Consent of the Lords Spiritual and Temporal, and Commons, in this present Parliament assembled, and by the Authority of the same, That the Mayor of *Arundel* for the Time being, the Senior Burgess of *Arundel* for the Time being, Names of the Commissioners.

3 X 2

The Preamble of the Littlehampton Harbour Act, 1732, which provided for a new mouth to the river to be cut and the erection of piers.

Introduction

The river Arun is the longest river in Sussex. It rises in St Leonards Forest near Horsham and flows thirty-seven miles to the English Channel at Littlehampton. The lower reaches have been used for moving goods and chattels since the Norman Conquest and the river was made navigable as far as Stopham Bridge during the reign of Queen Elizabeth I. By 1637 the navigation had been extended to Pallingham Quay and would have advanced farther if the bill, introduced into the House of Lords four years later to link the rivers Wey and Arun, had become law.

Improvements made to Littlehampton Harbour in the seventeenth century led to gun boats being built and ships of 100 tons riding at anchor seven miles upstream at Arundel. A new harbour entrance and further work was carried out under the 1732 Act but it was not until 1785 that a serious attempt was made to improve the river above Houghton. The Arun Navigation Act authorised £10,000 to be raised to enable the company to build a $4\frac{1}{2}$ mile canal from Pallingham to Newbridge and for the five miles of twisting river between Greatham and Pulborough to be avoided by means of the two mile Coldwaltham Cut, which included a 375 yard long tunnel at Hardham. Incidentally this was the only tunnel to be built in Great Britain linking two sections of a river navigation. The cost of the canal and the tunnel was the substantial sum of £16,000. Burdened by debt, the company was rescued from liquidation by the third earl of Egremont, who purchased a 36 per cent shareholding in 1796. He was also the sole proprietor of the Rother Navigation, which had opened from Stopham to Midhurst in 1795. In 1804 the Arun Navigation company decided to erect docks for the repair and building of barges at Pallingham, work which hitherto had to be done at Pulborough.

The opening of the Wey & Arun Junction Canal, from Newbridge to Shalford in Surrey in 1816, and the Portsmouth & Arundel Canal in 1823, enabled improvements to be made to the Arun Navigation in the early 1820s. Consequently traffic increased from 17,600 tons in 1810 to 26,500 tons in 1824 and 36,000 tons in 1839. These figures do not, however, include the traffic to and from Arundel. In 1824 Littlehampton handled nearly 7,000 tons, whereas

Portrait of the third earl of Egremont (1751-1837) as a young man c.1775 (courtesy of Thos Agnew & Sons Ltd, London). After building the Rother Navigation to Midhurst in 1791-4 at his own expense, he became the principal shareholder in the Arun Navigation Company in 1796.

Below: This 1790 plan indicates the importance of the feeder stream from Amblehurst which supplied the Arun Canal above Lording's Lock, Wisborough Green and shows the circuitous route of the river by Pulborough which caused Hardham Tunnel to be built.

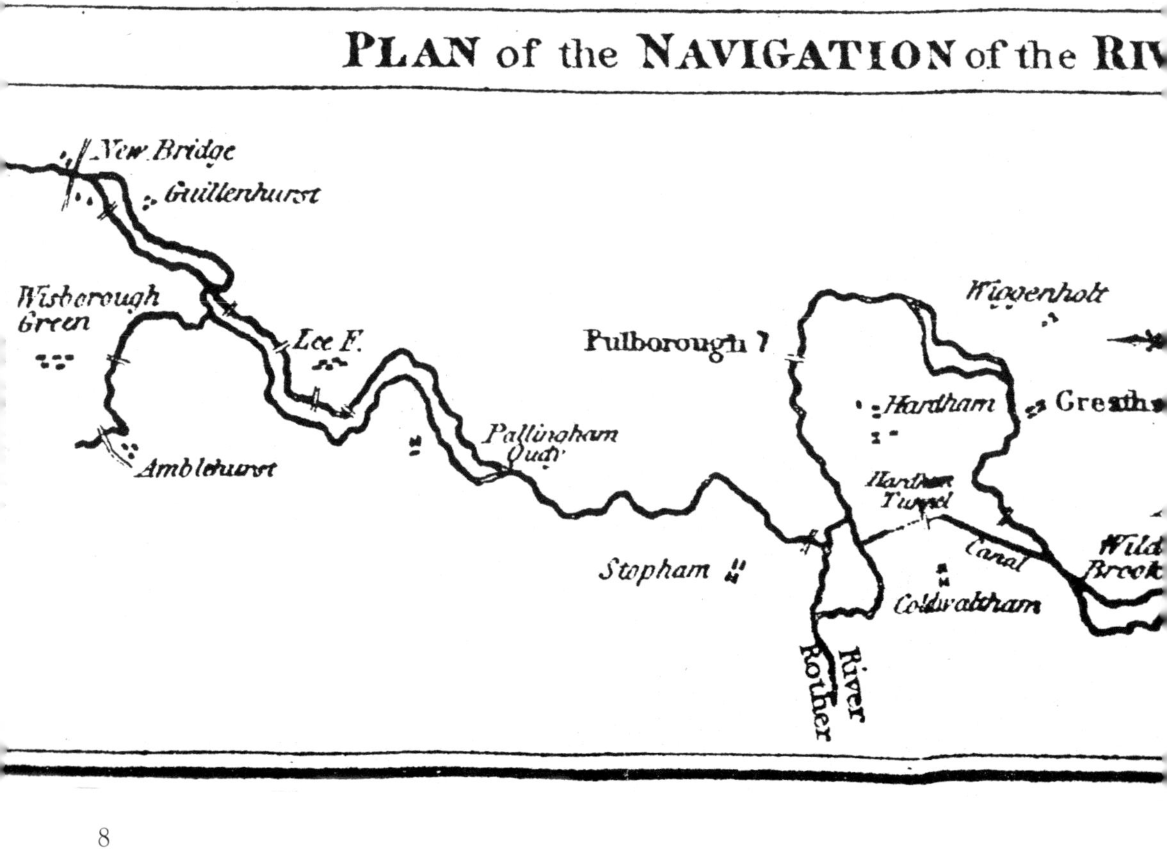

PLAN of the NAVIGATION of the RIV

New Bridge

Guillenhurst

Wisborough Green

Lee F.

Amblehurst

Pallingham Quay

Stopham

River Rother

Pulborough

Hardham

Hardham Tunnel

Canal

Coldwaltham

Wiggenholt

Greath

Wild Brook

Arundel managed over 45,000. Between 1831 and 1833 port dues paid at Arundel were three times those at Littlehampton.

Throughout the 1830s the Arun was a busy and successful navigation with a regular service of barges trading between London and Arundel and providing collections from, and deliveries to, Chichester, Pulborough, Petworth, Midhurst, Godalming and Guildford. The navigation company paid an annual dividend of 11 or 12 per cent, and would have done better if the Portsmouth & Arundel Canal had not proved such a failure. For over forty years the annual tonnage exceeded 20,000, but with the opening of the railway from Horsham to Pulborough and Petworth in 1859 and to Arundel in 1863, waterborne trade began to decline rapidly. In 1865 only 5,000 tons were carried on the Arun Navigation. The final dividend of 1 per cent on the £100 shares was paid in 1874 and in spite of determined efforts to keep the waterway open, it was finally closed in 1888. A detailed account of the last days of the navigation will be found in 'London's Lost Route to the Sea' (see bibliography).

The tideway between Littlehampton and Pallingham, on which traffic paid no tolls, remained in commercial use until the late 1920s. The Strudwicks of Fittleworth, the Doicks of Pulborough and the Henlys of Bury were the last barge-masters on the navigation.

Until 1927 the river between Littlehampton and Arundel was the responsibility of the Commissioners of Arundel Port, as laid down in the Harbour Acts of 1732, 1793 and 1825. Their authority was then transferred to the Littlehampton Harbour Board. The stretch of river above Arundel came under the jurisdiction of the Commissioners of Sewers for the Rape of Arundel from 1644 until 1933 when the Arun Catchment Board was formed.

The formation of the Wey & Arun Junction Canal Society in 1970 (a trust since 1973) has

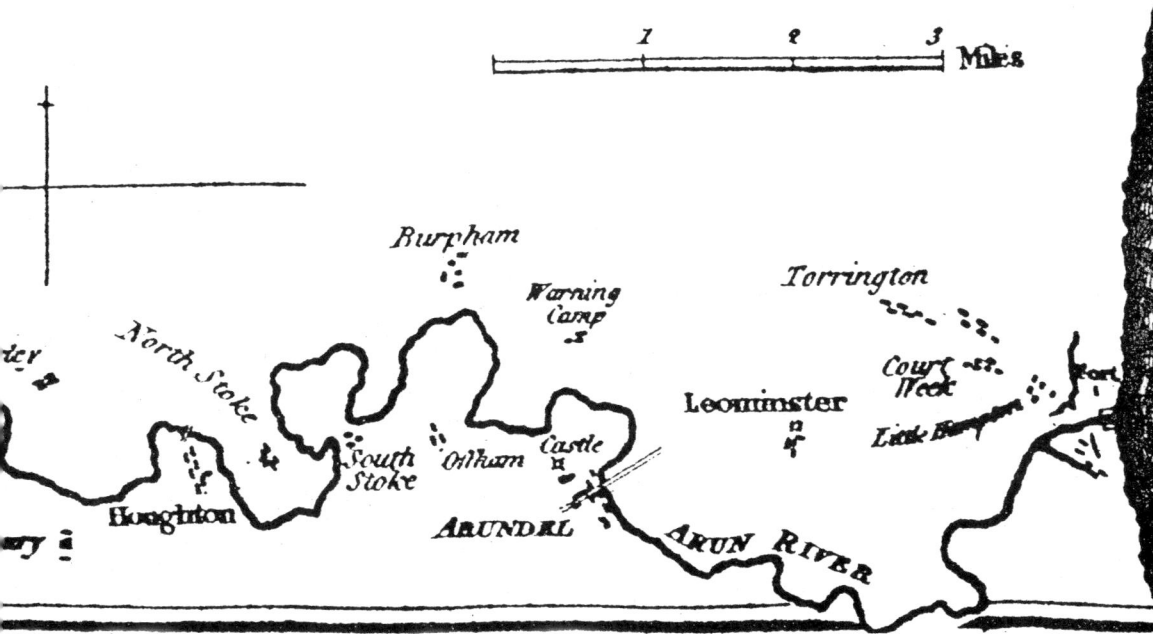

ARUN from the SEA to NEW BRIDGE .

THE RIVER ARUN

NAVIGATION

RIVER ARUN NAVIGATION INCORPORATED 25 GEO 3.d

TENDIMUS AD LATUM

COMPANY.

Share N°⸻

This is to Certify *that* ⸻
⸻
⸻

is a Proprietor of **ONE SHARE** *in the* **River Arun Navigation**, *numbered as above, and Registered in the Register Book of the Company, (subject to the Rules, Orders and Regulations of the said Company) and that he, his Executors, Administrators and Assigns are entitled to the Profits and Advantages thereof. Dated this ⸻ day of ⸻ 1842.*

MIDHURST

Clerk to the Company.

The capital of the Arun Navigation Company was £10,000, comprising one hundred shares of £100. By the late 1830s they were changing hands at £200 and paying an annual dividend of 12 per cent. Share certificates were not issued until 1842.

led to a resurgence of interest in the old waterway. By the year 2000 the trust had succeeded in clearing and dredging almost half of the eighteen miles of former canal bed, restoring seven locks to working order and rebuilding numerous bridges and culverts.

Public cruises now (July 2000) operate along a two mile stretch of waterway between Loxwood and Drungewick every weekend during the summer months and work has already commenced on reconstructing the road bridge and fallen aqueduct at Drungewick. When this has been completed, it should not be long before the navigation can be extended to Newbridge.

The next stage will then be to reopen the Arun Canal. Already two of the three lock chambers have been renovated, several bridges reconstructed and culverts repaired.

Once the Arun Canal has been restored from Newbridge to Pallingham, pleasure craft will be able to descend with the tide to Arundel and Littlehampton. It may even be possible one day for Hardham Tunnel to be reopened. Until that time efforts must be made to ensure its survival as a unique example of eighteenth century enterprise.

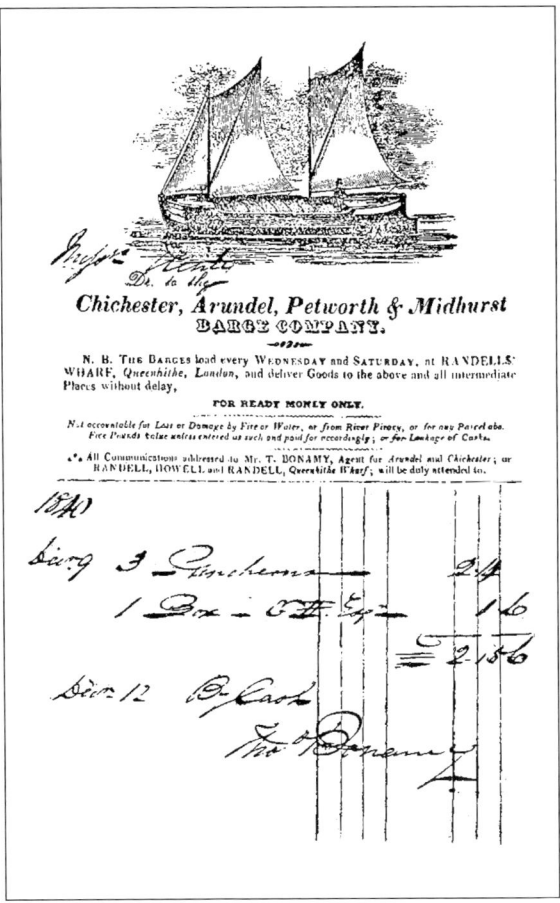

Invoice issued by Chichester, Arundel, Petworth & Midhurst Barge Company in 1840 and signed by Thomas Bonamy of Arundel.

RIVER ARUN NAVIGATION,

(Twelve Miles)

Tolls to be Charged from the 1st of August, 1856.

UP TOLLS.

		£	s.	d.
PER TON	Coal, Culm, and Slate, from Arundel to the Wey ...	0	0	9
	Coal to Elmbridge Wharf	0	0	9
	Ditto to Drungwick and Loxwood	0	1	8
	Ditto to Newbridge	0	1	8
	Culm to ditto	0	1	3
	Seed Cake and Corn to ditto	0	2	0
PER KILN	Lime to ditto	0	6	0
PER TON	Large Chalk to ditto	0	0	6
	Kiln ditto to ditto	0	0	4
	Chalk Grit, Flints, Gravel, and Sand to ditto	0	0	6
	Flint, and Stone for building, to ditto	0	1	0
	Lime and Soap Ashes	0	1	0
	Timber from Arundel to ditto	0	2	0
	Hoops, Bark, and Timber from Hardham, Stopham, and Pallingham to the Wey	0	1	0
	Hoops and Bark, Wharfage from Newbridge to the Wey	0	1	0
PER LOAD	Timber from Newbridge to the Wey, Wharfage and Drawing	0	2	6
PER HUN.	Spokes, Wharfage	0	0	6
PER TON	Merchandize Goods from Arundel and the Rother into the Wey and Arun	0	1	0

		£	s.	d.
PER LOAD	Timber converted, &c., at Newbridge Wharf	0	1	0
PER TON	Storing and delivering Cake, Manure, &c., at Newbridge Store	0	1	0
	Bark stored at Newbridge Wharf for every entire 3 months and for any less period than 3 months	0	1	0
	For shooting and Storing Bark	0	1	0
	For Stored Bark, to pay on Delivery	0	1	0

RIVER ARUN NAVIGATION,

(Twelve Miles)

Tolls to be Charged from the 1st of August, 1856.

DOWN TOLLS.

	£	s.	d.
PER TON Merchandize Goods from the Wey and Arun to the Rother or Arundel	0	1	0
Timber, Plank, &c. from the Wey to Arundel ...	0	1	0
Ditto from Elmbridge, Compasses, Tickner's Heath, and Jinnets	0	1	0
Ditto from Drungwick and Loxwood	0	1	6
Ditto from Newbridge Wharf, including Wharfage and Drawing	0	2	6
Posts and Rails from Newbridge	0	2	0
Malt and Corn from ditto	0	2	0
Bark or Hoops from ditto	0	2	0
Ditto from Loxwood	0	2	0
For all Goods brought from the Wey and Arun, and Landed at Newbridge Wharf	0	1	0
Hoops from the Rother, or elsewhere, stacked at Newbridge Wharf	0	1	0

TUNNEL TOLLS.

	£	s.	d.
PER TON Passing to and fro, including Coldwaltham Brook ...			
Timber, Bark, Hoops, Coal, Culm, Corn, Lime, and Merchandize Goods	0	0	6
Large Chalk	0	0	4
Kiln Chalk, Grit, Ashes, &c.	0	0	3
Stone for Building	0	0	6
Stone, Flint, Gravel for Roads, Sand, and all Kinds of Manure	0	0	3
Corn to Hardham Mill	0	0	3

JAMES POWELL,

Clerk.—

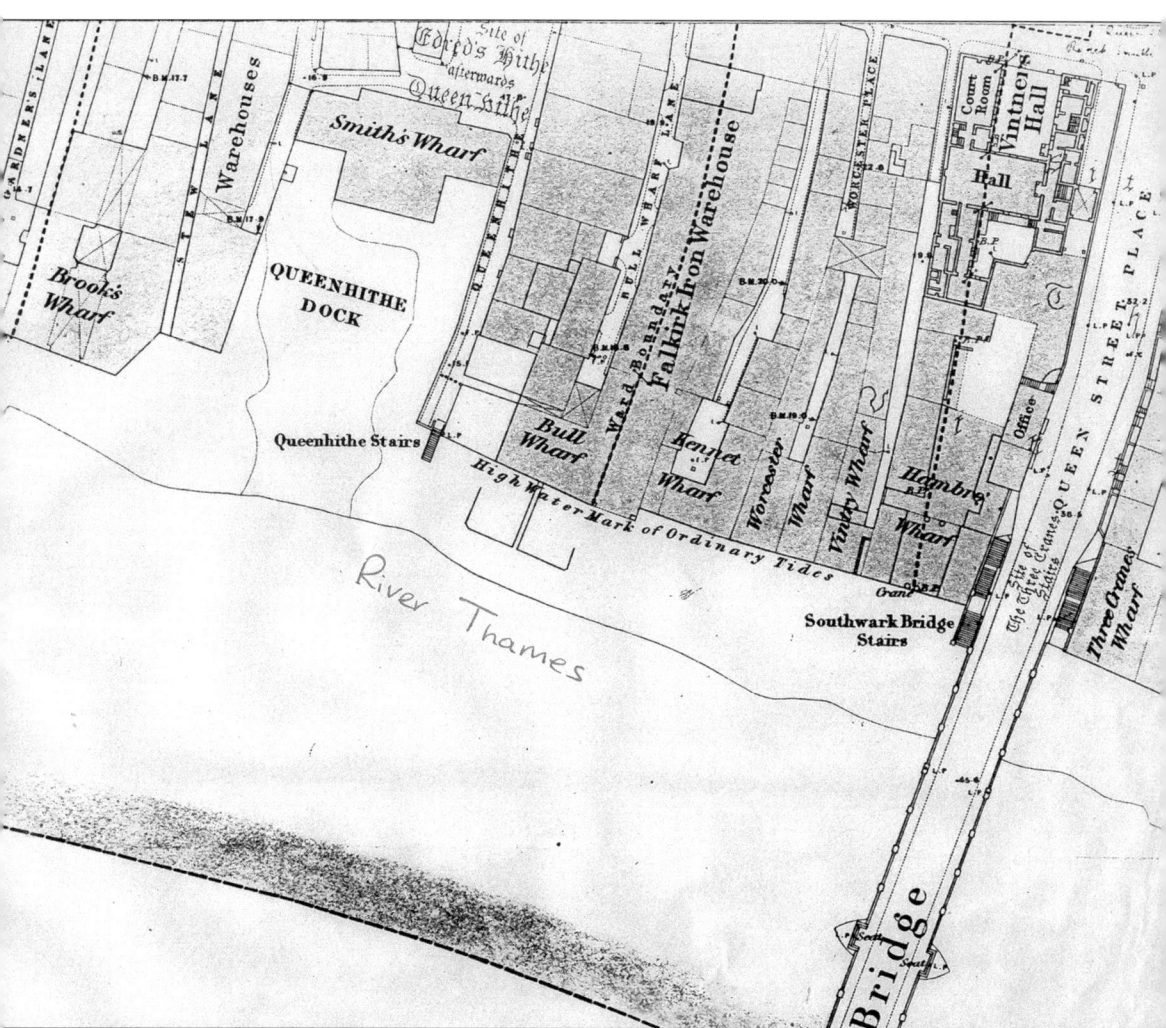

Plan of the wharves lying above Southwark Bridge, 1875. Barges were advertised in the 1830s as regularly leaving Queenhithe, Brooks and Three Cranes Wharf for Arundel, Chichester and Portsmouth whether loaded or not.

FOR CONVEYANCE OF GOODS OF EVERY DESCRIPTION TO AND FROM
LONDON, BY CANAL.

212

To Seward and Co.

N.B.—The Barges load every Saturday, at RANDELL's WHARF, Queenhithe, London, and
deliver Goods to Portsmouth, Portsea, Gosport, Isle of Wight, &c. &c. without delay.
FOR READY MONEY ONLY.
AGENTS:—T. Bonamy, 30, Lombard Street, Portsmouth; W. H. Bonamy, Chichester; S. Tobitt,
Arundel; Randell and Co., Queenhithe Wharf, London.

Seward & Co invoice, 1830, for conveyance of goods to and from London by canal.

15

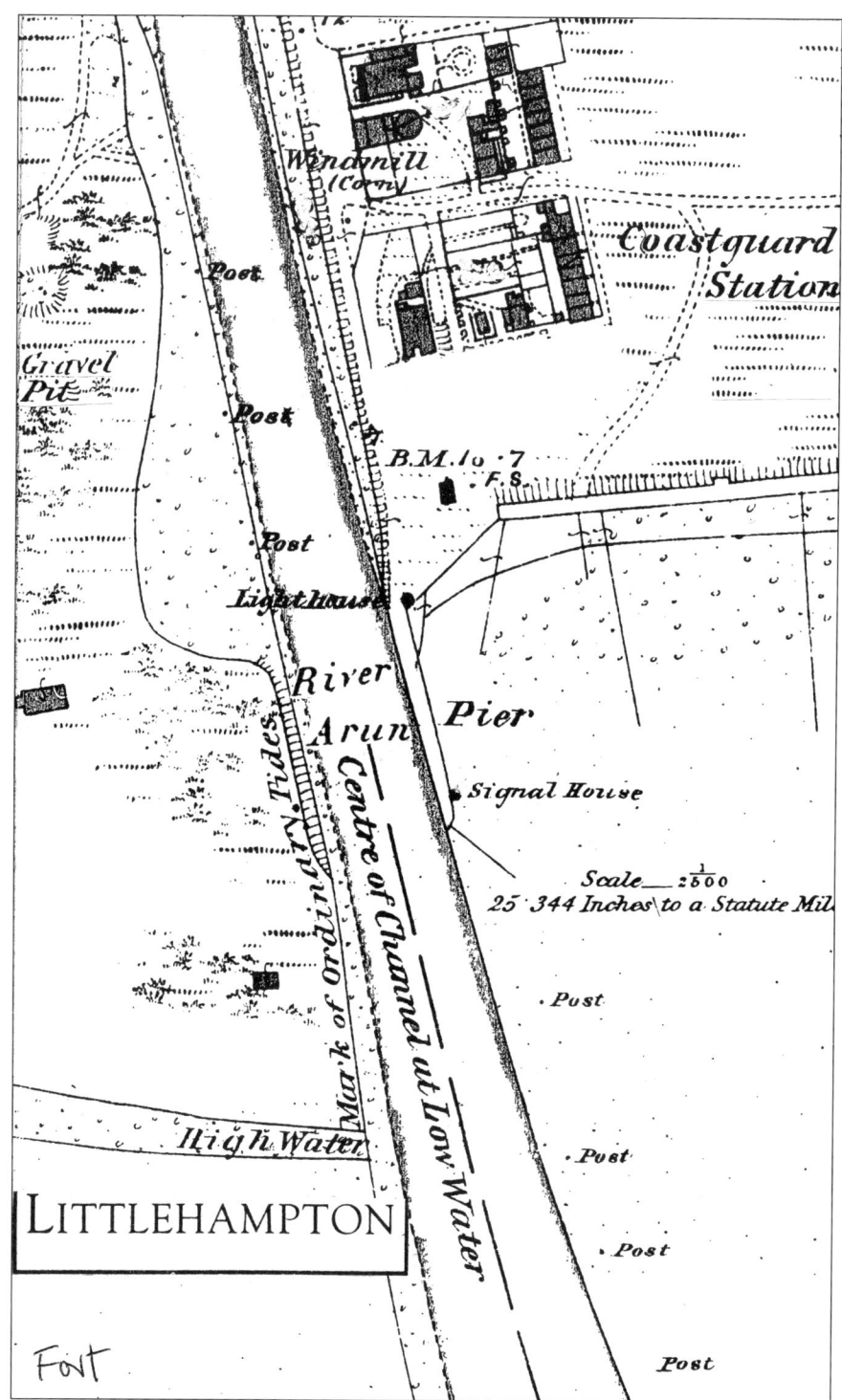

Map of entrance to Littlehampton Harbour, 1876. [25 inches: 1 mile]. It is interesting to note that for security reasons the identity of the black square (i.e. the fort built in 1854), shown above the High Water Mark, is omitted.

One
Littlehampton Harbour

The mouth of the river Arun and entrance to Littlehampton Harbour, c.1820. This painting by William Daniell (1769-1837) was published in his four volume series A *Voyage round Great Britain*. The building visible behind the east pier was the officers' quarters, built in connection with the battery erected in around 1759 (now the Mound).

A contemporary engraving of Littlehampton fort, pier and lighthouse in 1861. The fort had been built on the west bank of the river in 1854. Its armament consisted of three 68 and two 32-pounder cannons. In 1870 its effectiveness as a defence work was considered obsolete and the War Office recommended its reconstruction. However, nothing was done. The guns were removed in 1891 and the fort partially dismantled. During the Second World War the former magazines beneath the ramparts were used by the military for storage; today only the stone facing to the entrance and the outer walls and earthworks remain visible.

The view looking east shows the beach front terrace and two distant windmills.

Previous page: The first pier at Littlehampton was completed in 1735, but the build up of shifting sand over the years required the pier and break-waters to be extended. Acts of Parliament passed in 1793 and 1825 enabled this work to be carried out. This painting by Augustus Callcott (1779-1844), engraved by J. Cousen, shows the old pier in around 1810.

The paddle tug *JUMNA* towing a brigantine out of the river *c*.1900. The *JUMNA* served the Commissioners of the Port of Arundel from 1884 until 1921. On the right stands the pepper pot lighthouse, built in 1848 but removed during the Second World War, and the windmill built in 1831 by Henry Martin, a Bognor miller. The mill ceased working in 1913 and was demolished to make way for Butlin's enlarged fun fair in 1932.

Mussel Row Cottages in Pier Road on the left, and the windmill in 1874. The cottages were built in around 1800 for the use of local watermen who formed part of the oyster fleet. In 1929 the row was rebuilt and now houses a line of cafés and shops.

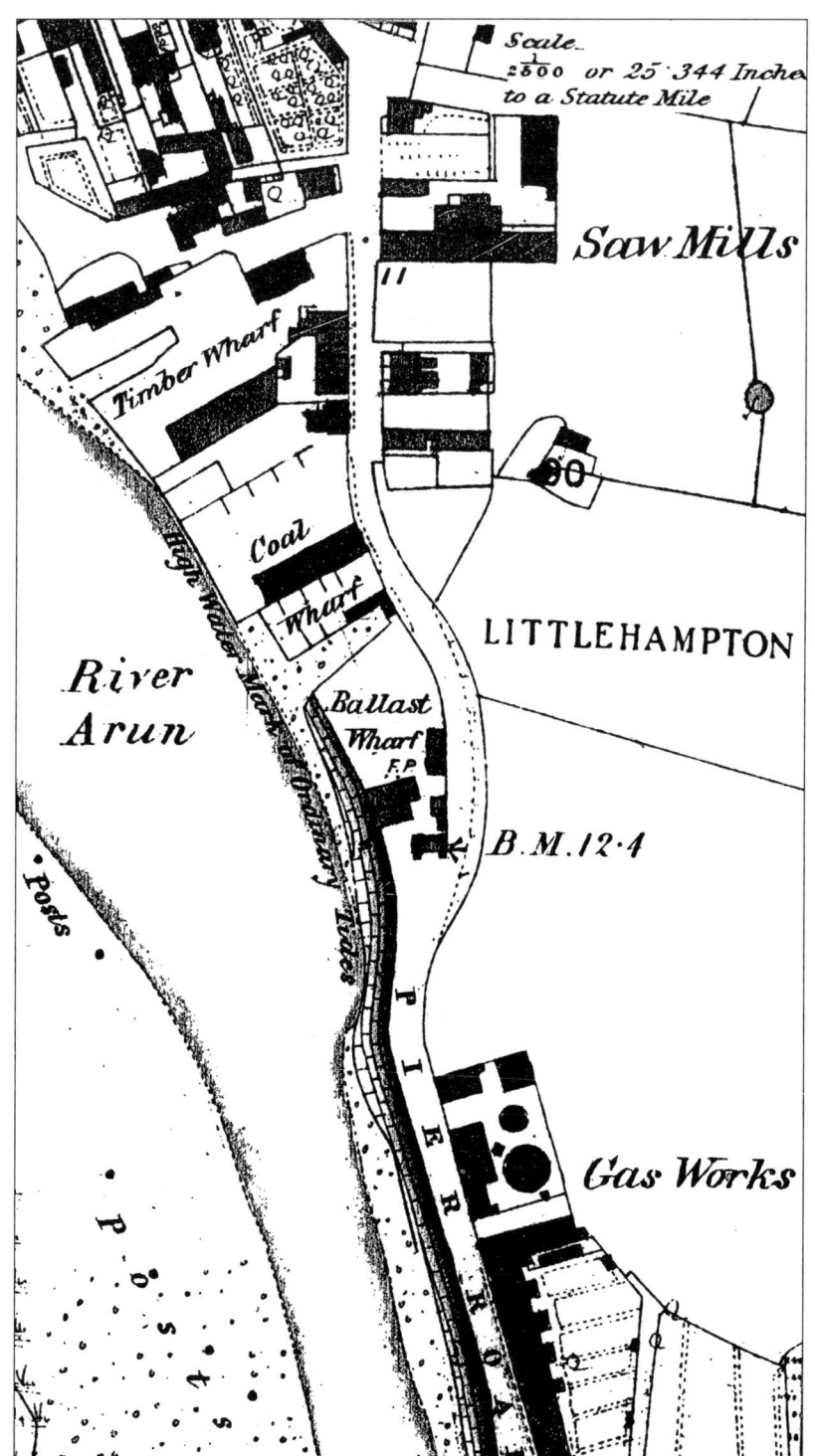

In the 1870s Pier Road was one of the most significant of local thoroughfares with its wharves on one side and the saw mills and gas works on the other. The gas works had been established in 1847 and were relocated at the turn of the century. [25 inch survey, 1876].

The Ockenden family were well-known ironmongers in Littlehampton, whose premises in River Road were built on the site of Thomas Isemonger's shipyard. The warehouses seen here were once aircraft hangers, brought in 1922 from the war-time American airfield on the Rustington Sea Estate.

A view of merchant shipping moored by the wharves in Pier Road at the turn of the nineteenth century. In the background can be seen the tall square chimney of Constable's Anchor Brewery, built in 1871 and demolished in 1972.

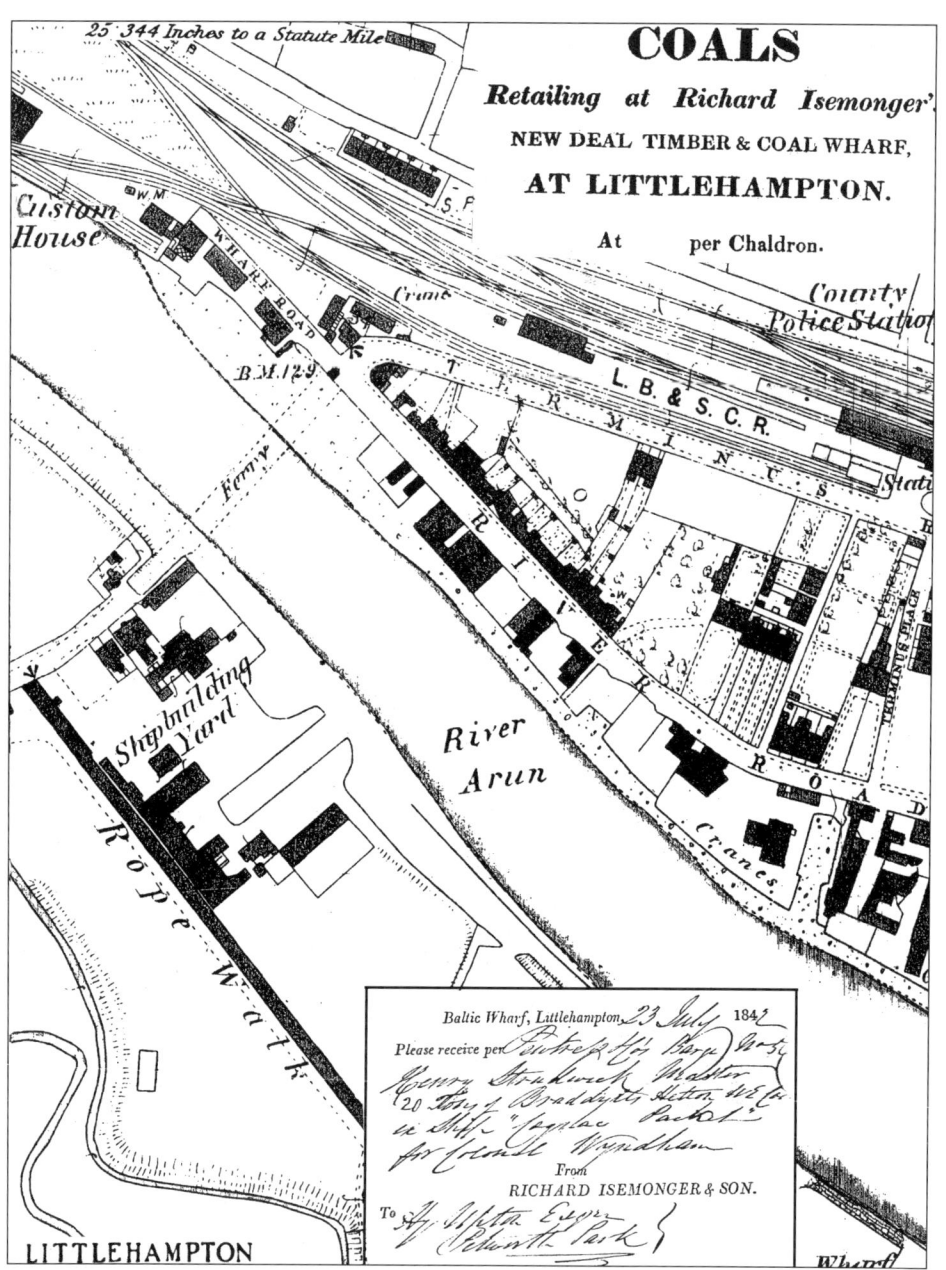

Within the map/image:

COALS

Retailing at Richard Isemonger'

NEW DEAL TIMBER & COAL WHARF,

AT LITTLEHAMPTON.

At   per Chaldron.

25·344 Inches to a Statute Mile

Custom House

County Police Station

Crane

L. B. & S. C. R.

T E R M I N U S

B.M.129

Ferry

R I V E R

Shipbuilding Yard

River Arun

Rope Walk

Cranes

R O A D

LITTLEHAMPTON

Baltic Wharf, Littlehampton, 23 July 1842

Please receive per [...]
[...]
20 [...] of Braddyll's [...]
[...]

From
RICHARD ISEMONGER & SON.

The 1876 map shows the river ferry and the huge shipbuilding yard of Stephen Olliver. He had bought the land in 1837 and installed a slipway, ship repair yards, saw pits, a smithy and a ropery. Much of the timber used in the building of Aldershot barracks (1854-9) was barged from here via the Wey & Arun and Basingstoke Canals. On the opposite bank the Isemongers owned much of the property in River Road. Isemonger & Son's barges left from Chichester and Littlehampton two or three times a week bound for Three Cranes Wharf by Southwark Bridge. The bowsprits of ships docked in Thomas Isemonger's graving dock (marked from the 'OA' in Road to the river) used to overhang the roadway. In around 1890 the dock was filled in, but the tumbledown sheds and cranes remained standing until the 1920s. Inset is an 1842 delivery note for 20 tons of coal sent to Petworth by Richard Isemonger & Son.

Littlehampton Ferry had been authorised by an Act of Parliament in 1824 and opened in 1825. The ferry barge was operated by means of a windlass and chain and was capable of carrying two coaches with four horses apiece. Pleasure boater J.B. Dashwood recorded in July 1867 that on reaching Littlehampton he had been cautioned against the submerged chains of the floating bridge.

The wooden ferry barge had been built in Thomas Isemonger's River Road Shipyard in 1824 and remained in service until 1873 when it was replaced by a steel pontoon (seen here in around 1900) at a cost of £1,000.

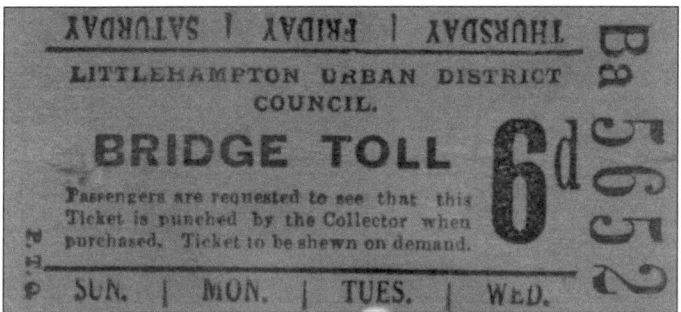

Various bridge toll tickets. The one penny toll (1923) could also be used for the little ferry from Pier Road to the golf club. The toll was reduced for foot passengers using the bridge to only 1/2d (1924). Vehicles paid 6d or 9d.

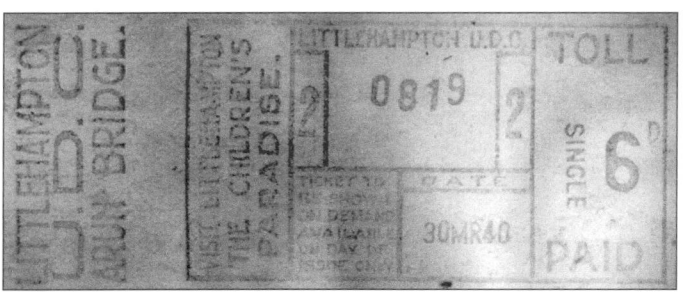

Interestingly, Littlehampton was still advertising the town as the 'Children's Paradise' in March 1940, less than two months before the cross channel evacuation from Dunkirk.

Littlehampton swing bridge in 1908. It continued in use for motor vehicles until 1973 when the new road bridge was opened. The swing bridge was dismantled in 1981 so that the present day footbridge with a retracting centrepiece could be constructed on its enormous piers.

Ford Lock looking toward Arundel as it appeared in around 1855. The Ford section of the Portsmouth & Arundel Canal had become virtually disused since the opening of the Shoreham to Chichester Railway in 1846 and had, according to Stanton, the lock-keeper at Bramley, not been used since 1856.

View from the river of the grass-covered bed of the canal in 1951. Ford Church is hidden at left by the clump of trees. The building at right marks the site of the old Engine House.

Two
Upstream to Ford

The entrance to the Portsmouth & Arundel Canal at Ford c.1840. In the background can be seen Ford road bridge and the huge three storey pump-engine house and tower.

Above and below: In 1862 the single track timber drawbridge was replaced by this double track lift and roll iron structure. Although this had a centre span of 90 feet, the width of the navigable passage was reduced to 40 feet. This bridge took half an hour or so to open as all the wires passing over had to be disconnected. Strengthened in 1898, it remained substantially unaltered until it was replaced by a fixed bridge in 1938.

Previous page, top: Ford railway bridge open for shipping, 1846. In spite of determined opposition from the Arun Navigation Proprietors, the London & Brighton Railway Company obtained its Act to build a line from Shoreham to Chichester, which involved throwing a drawbridge across the Arun at Ford. The telescopic bridge had a sixty foot opening which took two men and a boy at least five minutes to open. Delays in opening the bridge to river traffic led to claims for compensation. £5 was the usual fine paid for a 45 minute hold-up, but in April 1858 a delay of 1 hour 50 minutes to the steam tug and her tow, the brigatine *Arun*, resulted in £10 being paid.

Bottom: Ford railway bridge closed to shipping, 1846.

This view shows the tug *JUMNA* in 1910, moored by the double track lift and roll structure which had replaced the single track timber bridge in 1862.

In 1938 it was decided to replace it by a fixed bridge when the railway line was electrified. In this 1953 view the remains of the building which housed the men who had formerly to open the bridge can be seen.

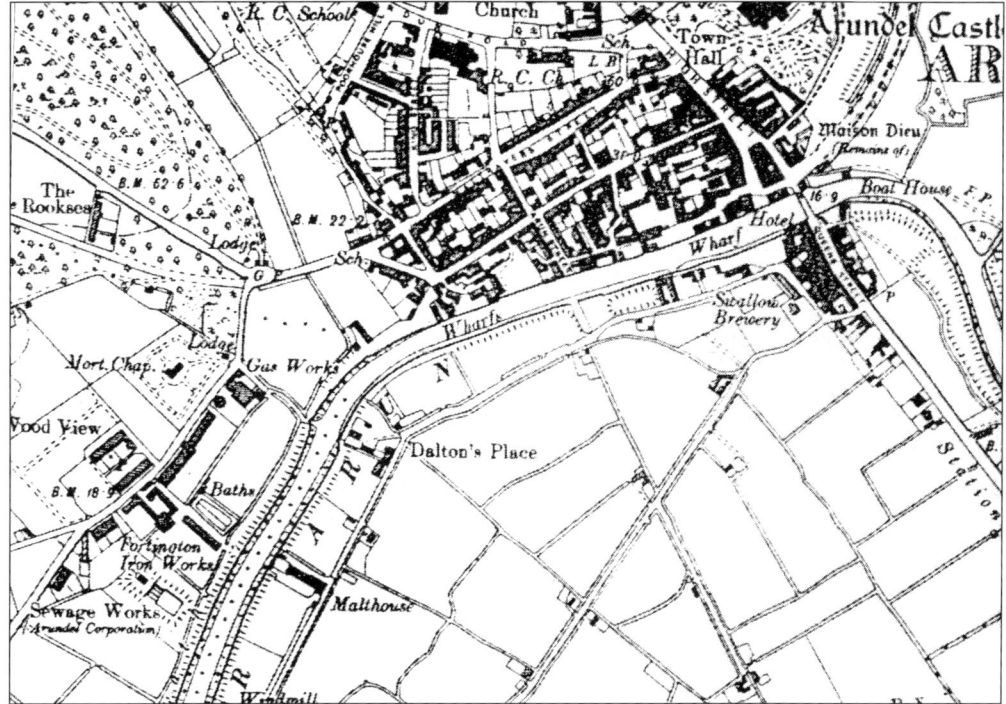

The six inch map issued in 1896 reveals the location of some of the main users of the navigation. They included the Arundel Gas Works built in the late 1830s, the Tortington Iron factory and the Swallow Brewery.

The gas works wharf *c*.1925. The Arundel Gas Light & Coke Company was founded in 1838 and was established along the Ford Road. In the nineteenth century much of the coal for the gas works was brought up by brigantines from the north-east of England. Later barges carried the coal from Littlehampton. The gas works were demolished soon after 1975.

Three
Ford to Arundel Docks

A sailing barge approaching Arundel, c.1900. The mast is set almost midway along her length with a spritsail of a good working size. The mate has to hand a long pole to ease her round the river bends, particularly where high banks shelter the sail and the inrushing tide takes charge. She is decked at bow and stern with small side decks and an open hold.

Nineteenth-century shipping scene depicting topsail schooners after a painting by L.A. Wilcox. South Marshes Mill was built in 1830 but ceased grinding corn after storm damage in 1915. The tower still stands today, forming part of a private dwelling.

Arundel remained a busy port until the early 1920s. This painting by Stuart Lloyd in 1899 shows the barge *Speedwell* of Arundel laden with timber and three coasters including the *Alice* of London and the *Mary* of Milton.

Arundel Castle and town in 1644, by which time it had become the chief timber-exporting port in south-east England. Hollar's engraving shows the wooden trestle bridge described in 1568 as the 'ancient one of great height and length'. It was replaced in 1724 by a stone bridge of three arches. In 1722 Daniel Defoe wrote that the town was decayed but that the timber shipped from there to Woolwich, Chatham and all the other naval dockyards was esteemed the best and largest brought by sea anywhere in England. The Admiralty also reported in 1728 that Arundel provided the best oak timber and was eminent for building hoys and ketches.

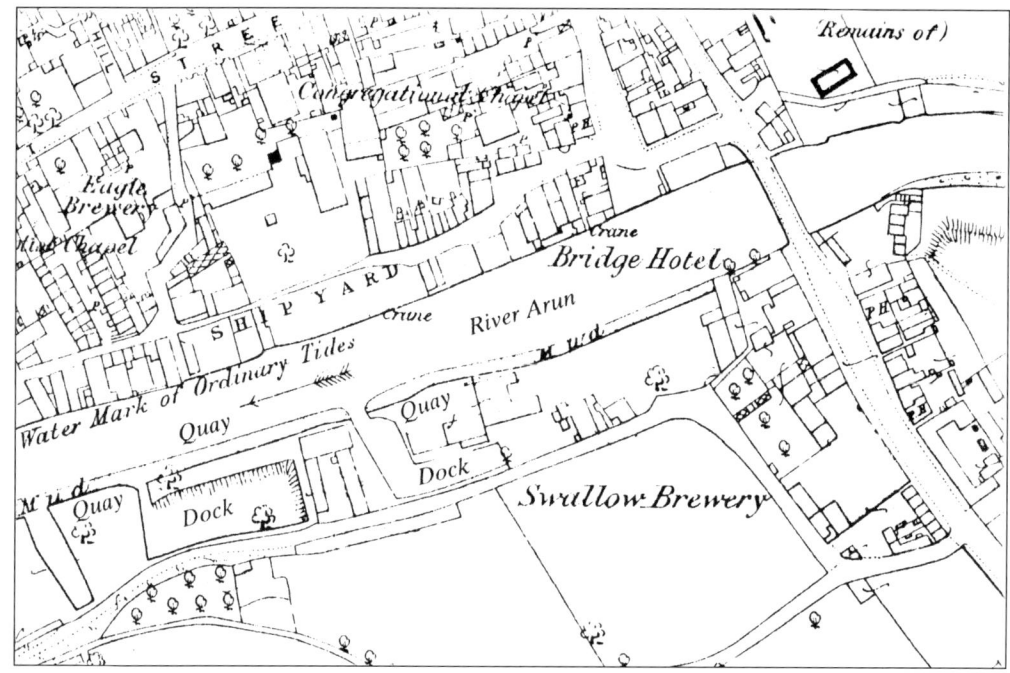

There were quays and docks on both sides of the river as far as the bridge, as indicated on the 25 inch 1875 ordnance survey.

The former busy shipyard was almost deserted when this photograph was taken in May 1893.

View of Arundel Docks *c*.1820. Note the shipyard and crane at left and the entrance to the docks at right.

By 1950, when this photograph was taken, the town quay had been replaced by a bus terminal.

Arundel Castle and Bridge.

In 1929 the former corn store at left was a factory making deck chairs and garden furniture, but the building was burnt down in July 1930 and not rebuilt.

Arundel Bridge.

The Bridge Hotel at right c.1905. This gracious Georgian coaching inn was formerly known as the Dolphin. During the rebuilding of the bridge in the 1930s the hotel collapsed when its foundations were swept away by the waters of what is the second fastest flowing river in England.

Four
Arundel to Houghton

Arundel in 1798. The post-mill at right was erected on Portreeves Acre in 1769. It was used for making cement in the mid-nineteenth century and was dismantled in the 1864.

John Constable's drawing of a barge lying aground in 1834 while awaiting repair at Arundel. Observe the post-mill at Portreeves Acre at right. The famous landscape artist died in 1837.

The post-mill at Portreeves Acre above Arundel Castle c.1850, after a painting by F.W. Watts (1800-1862). The mill was erected in 1769 and dismantled in 1864.

Here we see two different methods used to navigate the Arun in the early 1820s. Until the tow-path was built barges were either poled up or downstream with the tide or sailed. Later horse towage and steam power was also used. This engraving is by John Bailey after William Scott, 1818.

A South West View of **Arundel Castle, Sussex**, the seat of His Grace the **Duke of Norfolk**
Taken from the Brighton Road.

An engraving by Joseph Jeckes of Arundel Castle from the Brighton Road shows sailing barges in around 1810.

A later painting of Portreeves Mill in the early 1860s by Edwin Pettitt (1840-1912) shortly before it was demolished in 1864.

Hay barges were not common on the Arun Navigation, since hay was plentiful in the locality and there were few places nearby to which it could profitably be carried. This oil painting by Walter Caffyn, showing a hay raft lashed amidships, is dated 1878.

The Arun Catchment Board's maintenance barge moored above Arundel Castle, 1923. This bend of the river has been one of the most painted scenes in Sussex.

The same scene painted by Alfred East (1849-1913) towards the close of the nineteenth century.

WINDMILL NEAR ARUNDEL.

Mr William Atfield's cement mill, built in 1861, stood 150 yards upstream of the post-mill which was demolished in 1864. This mill was burnt down in 1892.

Barges were normally sailed or poled downstream with the ebbing tide, but against the current it was necessary for horse towage to be used above Arundel, as depicted in this watercolour by Henry Charles Fox (1860-1925) which was painted around the turn of the century.

Sailing barge approaching Arundel Castle in 1830. The eight foot tow-path between Houghton and Burpham, begun in 1821, was not completed to Arundel until later in the century.

W.H. Mason's 1870 watercolour showing the Black Rabbit alehouse established in 1793 at centre and the Amberley Chalk pits. The river is to the right of the drainage channel in the foreground.

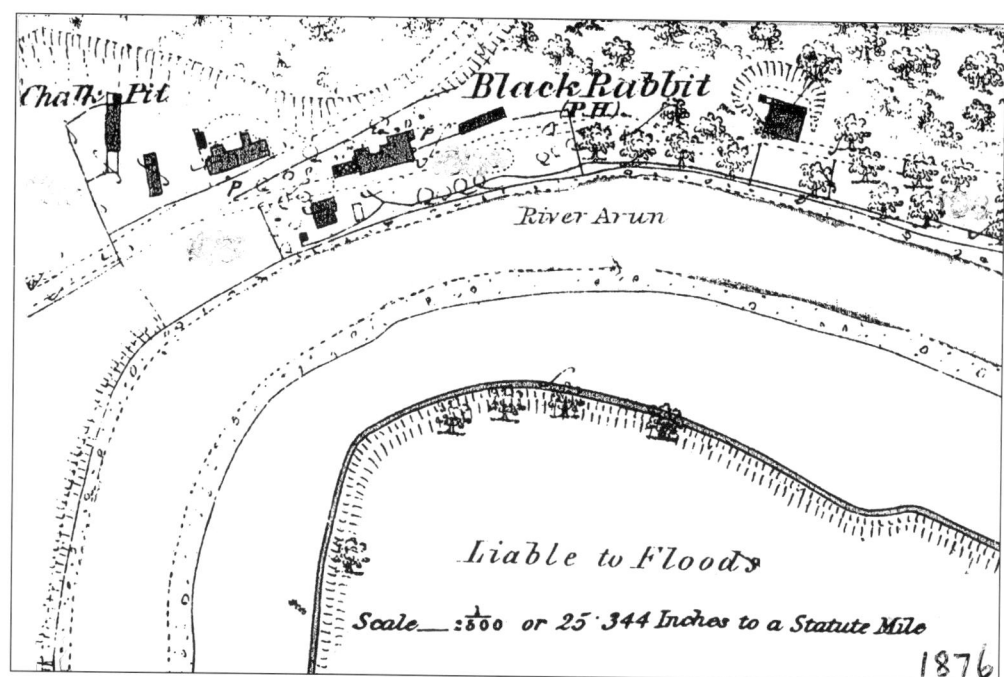

The Black Rabbit Inn at Offham was originally a row of cottages. It has been a popular riverside pub for over two centuries, with rowing skiffs and gigs for hire. The chalk quarry at the rear was begun when the Offham cut was made in 1861-2 and was in use until the 1970s.

Postcard *c.*1925, showing wooden skiffs moored in the tideway with the chalk pits in the background.

A chalk barge moored below the Black Rabbit *c.*1900. The river Arun was banked with raw chalk blocks which eroded and had to be regularly replaced. The chalk was brought up and down from the Black Rabbit in barges propelled by long poles operated by men who walked, pushing from bow to stern along narrow decks on the gunwales.

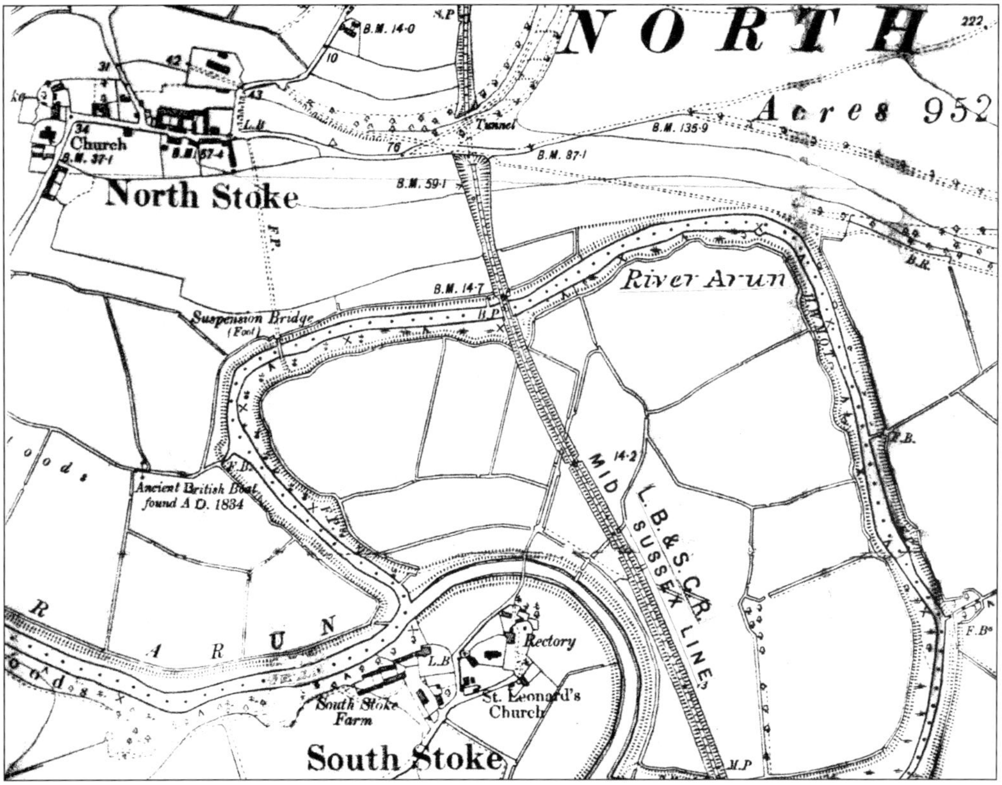

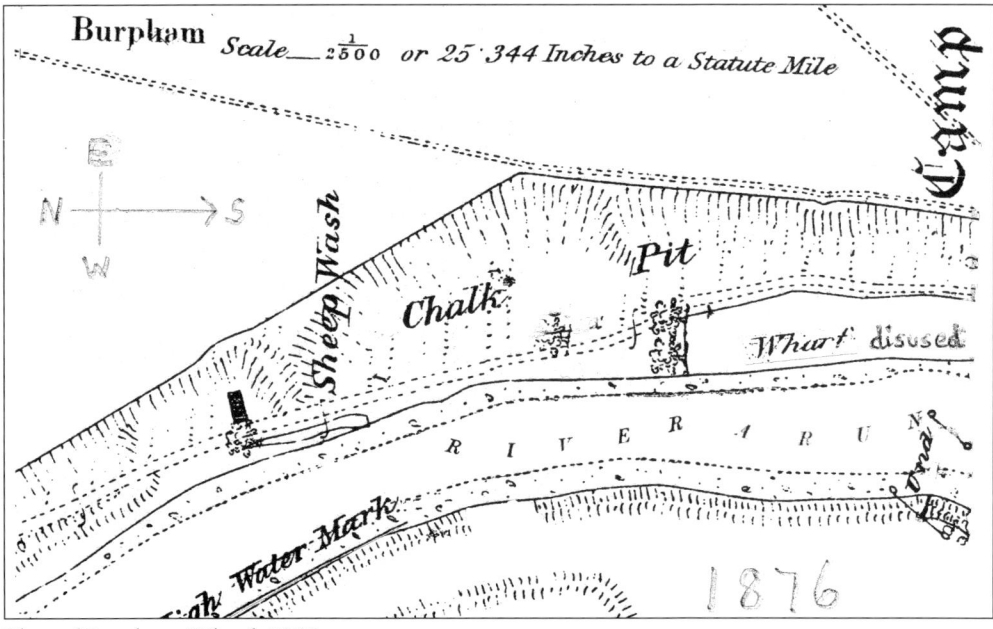

In an attempt to alleviate the floods which plagued the Arun Valley, the Commissioners of Sewers made what became known as the 'horseshoe cut' at South Stoke in 1839. This shortened the navigation by over one mile but only slightly reduced the flooding. A plan to build a fresh cut to Houghton Bridge was abandoned because the consent of the landowners could not be obtained.

Plan of Burpham Wharf, 1876.

After the closure of the old chalk pit at Burpham the former wharf was used for harvesting and bundling osiers. The osiers used for basket making grew along the river bank and were stacked together with reeds for thatching, as seen in this 1910 view.

An oil painting by W.H. Mason of Burpham Wharf by moonlight c.1860. After the building of the fixed railway bridges across the river in 1862 barges would have had to unship their masts going to and from Burpham.

Burpham c.1910.

Author Robert Goodsell is seen a little further downstream from where the view above was taken in the early 1950s. An old landing craft or Motor Torpedo Boat, to which a superstructure had been added, was moored against the wooded left bank.

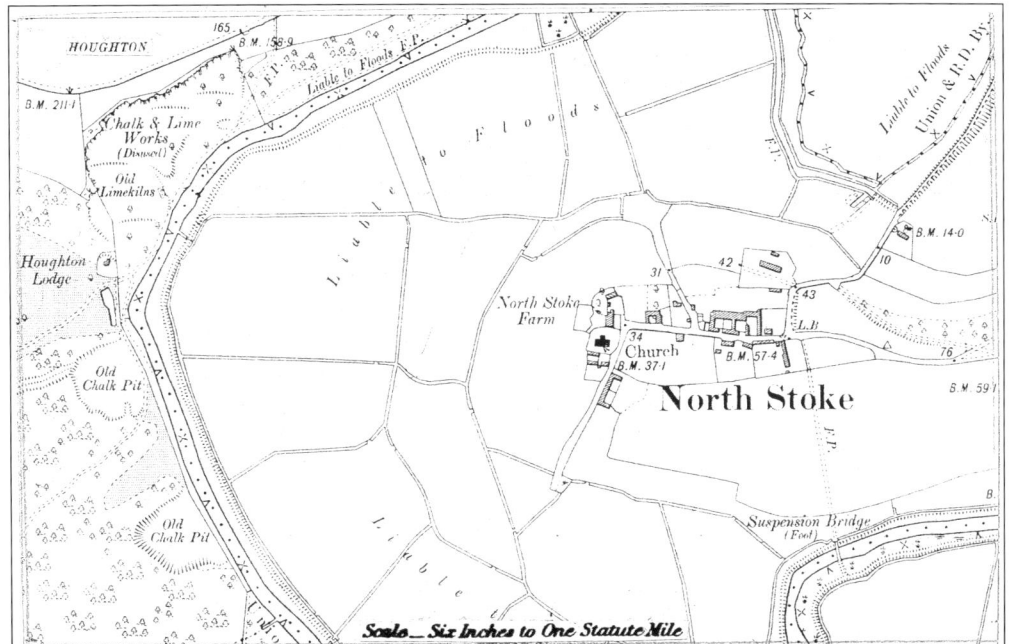

During the nineteenth century a series of chalk pits were cut from the cliffs at Houghton, whose produce could be moved by water to the riverside kilns at Pulborough and along the upper reaches of the Arun. This 1910 ordnance map shows the location of the disused chalk and lime works on the Duke of Norfolk's estate.

Drawing of the lime kilns opposite North Stoke, 1889.

The view of the chalk pits as one ascends the river between North Stoke and Houghton. Countryside explorers will find remains of lime kilns hidden beneath the dense foliage.

The chalk pit behind Amberley Station looking east is seen in about 1904. In front is the 350 yard cut built by Lord Egremont in 1802-3 from the river south of Houghton Bridge, to enable barges to moor as close as possible to the chalk pits he had developed on land he had bought in 1800. Arthur Young, writing in 1808, reported that Houghton pit was supplying some 40,000 tons of chalk annually, much of which was carried up the Arun to the kilns at Pulborough and Newbridge and to the Rother Navigation.

Amberley wharves and chalk pits, 1875. The cut was used in conjunction with the railway (opened in 1863) and was maintained until the outbreak of war in 1914.

In this 1951 illustration a barge, one of two abandoned in 1914, is seen lying in the cut.

ANNO VICESIMO QUINTO

Georgii III. Regis.

C A P. C.

An Act for amending and improving the Navigation of the River *Arun*, from *Houghton Bridge*, in the Parish of *Houghton*, in the County of *Sussex*, to *Pallenham Wharf*, in the Parish of *Wisborough Green*, in the said County; and for continuing and extending the Navigation of the said River *Arun*, from the said Wharf called *Pallenham Wharf*, to a certain Bridge, called *New Bridge*, situate in the Parishes of *Pulborough* and *Wisborough Green*, in the said County of *Sussex*.

WHEREAS the amending and improving the Navigation of the River Arun, in the County of Sussex, through the several and respective Parishes of Houghton, Amberley, Bury Wiggenholt, Coldwaltham, Greatham, Hardham, Pulborough and Stopham, in the said County, would be found very beneficial, and of great Utility to the Publick: *Preamble.*

24 T 2 And

Preamble to the 1785 Arun Navigation Act which authorised the improvement of the navigation of the tideway from Houghton Bridge to Jupp's Mead, Pallingham and the building of the canal to Newbridge. The Act also enabled a new cut to be made from Greatham Brook to Hardham for vessels drawing 3 foot 1 inch water.

Five
Amberley to Pulborough

Houghton Wharf, looking south *c*.1905. In the background are the quarries of Pepper & Sons' limeworks, which today are the site of the Chalk Pits Museum. Among a wide variety of industrial exhibits, there is a display of local canal relics.

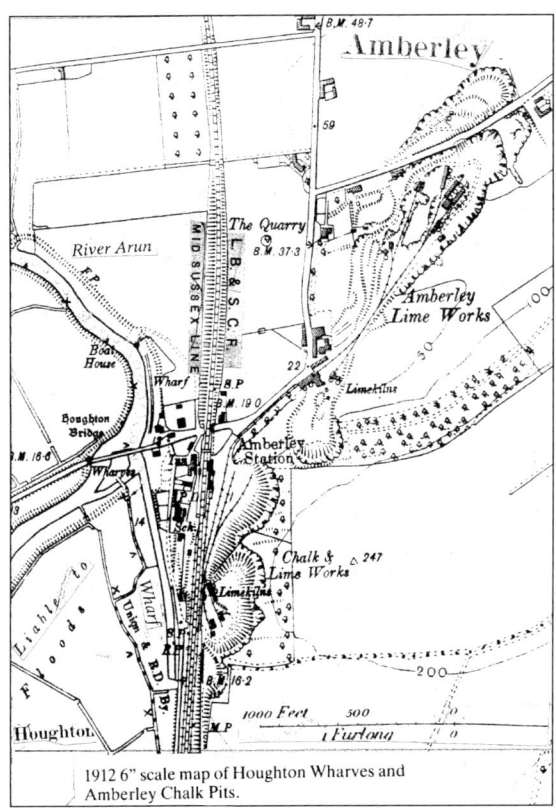

1912 six inch scale map of Houghton Wharves and Amberley Chalk Pits. Lord Egremont's cut is clearly marked ti the left of the railway station.

1912 6" scale map of Houghton Wharves and Amberley Chalk Pits.

Unloading a coal barge at Houghton Wharf c.1910.

On 20 October 1910 the *West Sussex Gazette* reported that Pepper & Sons' coal barge, *No. 64*, laden with 60 tons of coal, had shipped too much water and sunk at its moorings at Houghton Wharf. Numbering was a relic of the Arun Navigation's system of licensing. On the Wey Navigation barges were known by their names. In 1830 those of the Arundel Barge Company were listed as *Arun*, *Commerce*, *Egremont*, *Norfolk*, *Sovereign*, *Swallow* and *Union*.

HOUGHTON BRIDGE.

A drawing by Frank Baker of Houghton Wharf and Bridge *c*.1905.

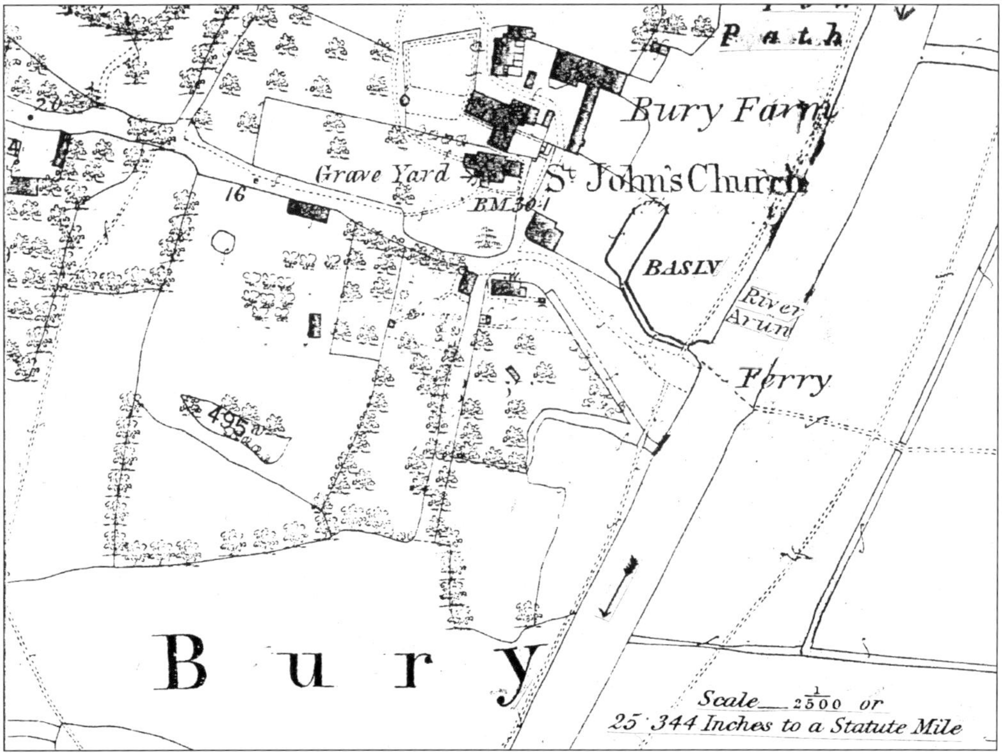

The 1876 survey of Bury shows the basin built between the church and the river for the repair of barges. Stop gates at the southern end allowed the pound to be emptied at low tide and filled at high water.

George Henly, bargemaster on the Arun Navigation from the 1850s until 1898. His family had been engaged in bringing coal, sand and timber to Bury Wharf for the best part of a century, and continued carrying until the late 1920s when the advent of the motor lorry resulted in the demise of water traffic. The Henly family were extensive landowners in Bury, engaged in farming, working lime kilns, trading as coal merchants and owning a fleet of river barges.

Bury Wharf in around 1910, showing one of Henly's barges under repair. Barges could only be refloated at high water spring tides. In 1925 the Southdown Bus Company commenced services from Horsham to Littlehampton via Bury, and by 1930 the ubiquitous motor lorry had made barge work unprofitable. Henly sold his fleet of three barges and commercial use of the river above Arundel ceased. The skiff by the foot-bridge was the ferry boat which operated until 1957, taking pedestrians bound for Amberley across the river.

Bury Church.

This later view was taken in around 1920 after the basin had been infilled.

Pleasure boating during the First World War when boats could still be hired at Houghton Wharf. In the background stands Timberley bridge, built in 1862 by the London, Brighton & South Coast Railway when it extended its line from Pulborough to Arundel.

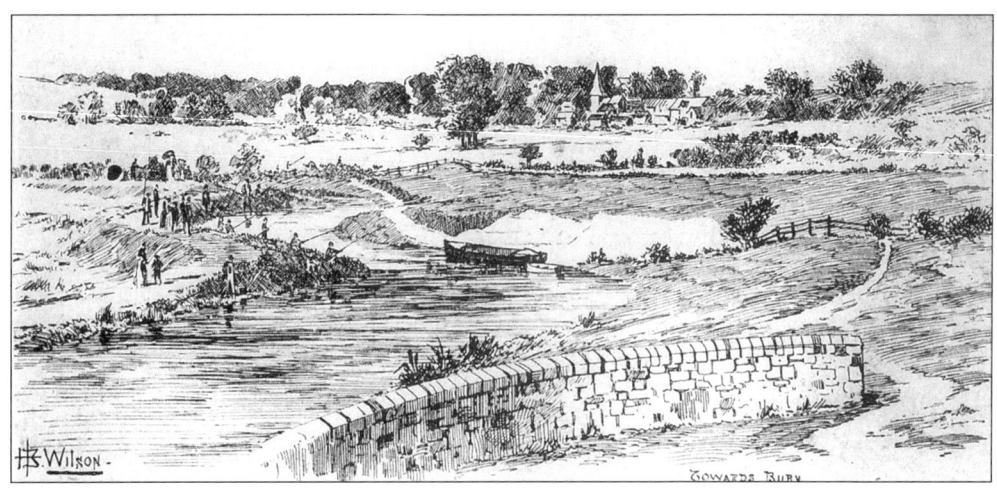

An 1889 drawing of the view from Amberley Wharf with Bury Church in centre background. Barges regularly brought up bolts of reeds and osiers from Burpham or Stoke for Pepper & Sons at Amberley and were then moored beyond the wharf to await cargoes of chalk for the lime kilns along the Rother Navigation and the upper reaches of the Arun.

J.B. Dashwood, voyaging with his wife and Pomeranian dog in a una boat from the Thames down the Arun Navigation in July 1867, remarked on the 'aggravating' kind of gates which could only be opened by pressing and holding the bars down to the ground while the animal stepped over. Apparently there were three or four of this type of fence along the tow-path to Houghton which gave them endless trouble. A passer-by suggested that the best plan was that practised by the bargeman, which was to blindfold the horse.

On the west bank between Timberley Railway Bridge and Greatham Bridge was the entrance to the Coldwaltham Cut, seen here in 1951. It has been blocked up by the river authority since 1970.

Greatham Bridge was built by Sir Henry Tregoz in the early fourteenth century. It was extended in the early part of the nineteenth century, but the iron section was not inserted until after floods had swept away part of the bridge in November 1838.

Bargemaster Sam Strudwick was one of the last carriers on the Arun Navigation. This view of the *Reliance* was taken in 1913. She was sold to the Arun Brick Company at Rackham in 1923 who moored her at Greatham Wharf. The brick works however failed, and in 1925 the Harbour Master at Littlehampton reported that it had been agreed that the abandoned barge should be given to the Commissioners of the Port of Arundel in return for its removal from the tideway.

Greatham Bridge.

No. 64 below Pulborough Bridge in 1898 with Bargemaster Henry Doick and his sons Percy and Tom. In the space of seven years (1895-1901) he made 521 voyages up and down the Arun, carrying 17,096 tons of cargo between Littlehampton and Pulborough. His average load was 33 tons, the maximum 38. The principal consignments were chalk, coal, culm, gravel and sand, but from time to time Doick carried ballast for Littlehampton brigs, steam coal for Arundel, bolts of reeds and osiers for Pepper & Son at Houghton, gas coal to Greatham and flints for the Duke of Norfolk at Timberley and for the Rector of Pulborough. Additional earnings arose from pile driving, and usually once or twice a year *No.64* was hired out to Mr Slaughter of York House School, Brighton, for barge parties to the Black Rabbit and picnics in South Woods. Doick delivered a barge load of coal to Greatham Wharf on 19 April 1902. It was to be his last. Six months later he died at the age of fifty-five.

A pre-Second World War view of the village of Pulborough. In 1931 the population was only 2,065, but by 1991 it had more than doubled. The meadows are now built over and even the chimney stacks at right which belonged to the Arun Hotel have vanished.

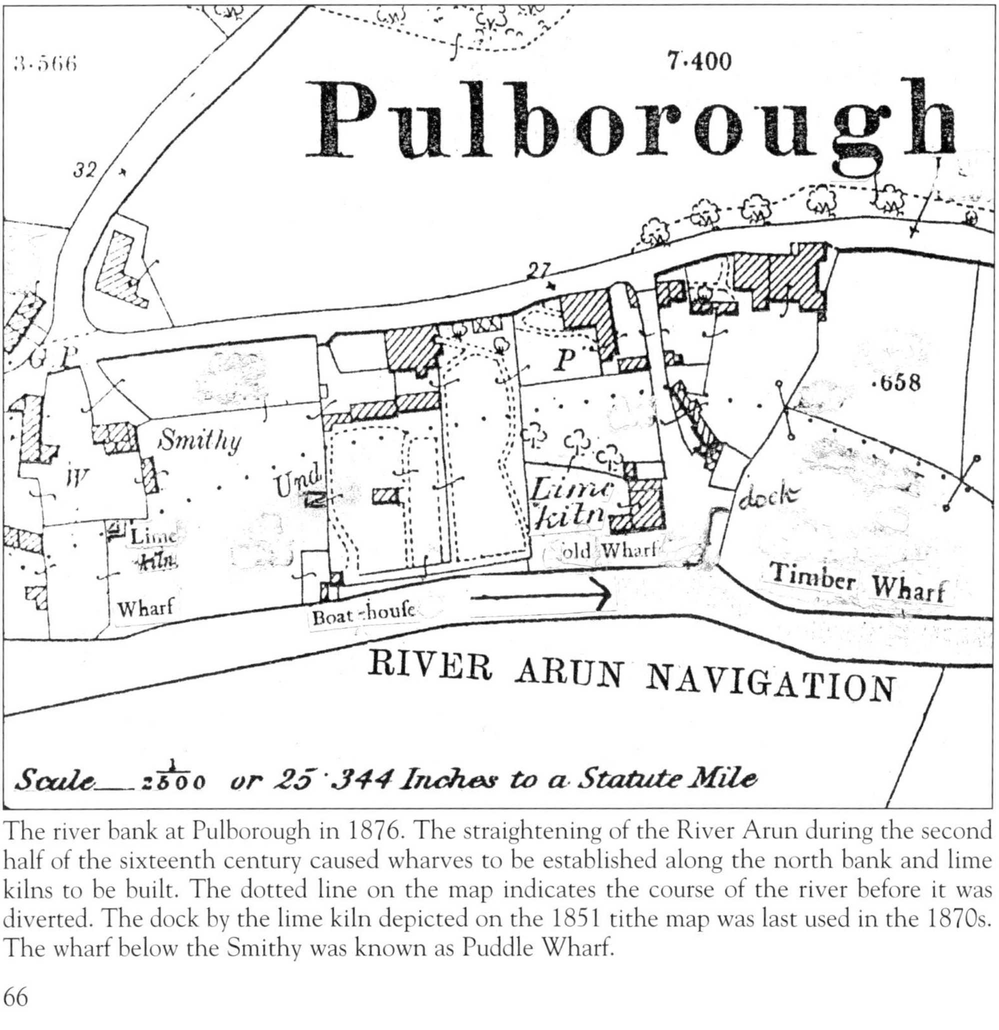

The river bank at Pulborough in 1876. The straightening of the River Arun during the second half of the sixteenth century caused wharves to be established along the north bank and lime kilns to be built. The dotted line on the map indicates the course of the river before it was diverted. The dock by the lime kiln depicted on the 1851 tithe map was last used in the 1870s. The wharf below the Smithy was known as Puddle Wharf.

This postcard of the river below Pulborough Bridge was sent on 4 June 1923 by Ian Bishop to his mother in south-west London to say that although he was having a good time, the heavy rain had swollen the river to $\frac{1}{4}$ mile wide so that 'the river's actual course was difficult to trace and most of the time they were sailing over fields'.

The substantial eighteenth-century lime kiln on the Old Wharf at Pulborough as seen in the 1930s. The stone lime kiln had two furnaces and measured 40ft x 30ft. On the east side was the dock which silted up in the 1870s (it is not marked on the 1876 survey). A few posts and piles remained in 1953. In June 1789 the Arun Navigation Company leased the old wharf from the devisees of Thomas Hampton for ninety-nine years at £6 per year, and in December 1804 the company agreed that Thomas Stone should maintain the wharf for the benefit of the bargemen.

Swan Bridge, Pulborough, originally a wooden structure downstream, was built in stone in around 1785. A fourth arch was added in 1834. Increasing road traffic caused the narrow bridge to be by-passed by the present bridge in 1936. This photograph, taken in 1921, shows the wooden boat-house at Templemead which survived the floods until 1940.

A late eighteenth-century water pavilion with chess board erected by Dr Peter Martin at Templemead. This view was taken in 1954 before a new boat-house was built on the west side of the building in 1958.

Six
Pulborough to Stopham

Swan Bridge, Pulborough, 1891. At centre left was the entrance to the cut which allowed barges to unload grain for the corn exchange, and there was also a dock on the left bank just above the bridge where barges could be repaired at low water. In the 1830s the Arundel Lighter Company's boats passed by daily to convey goods to London, Chichester and Portsmouth (Pigot's *Sussex Directory*, 1832).

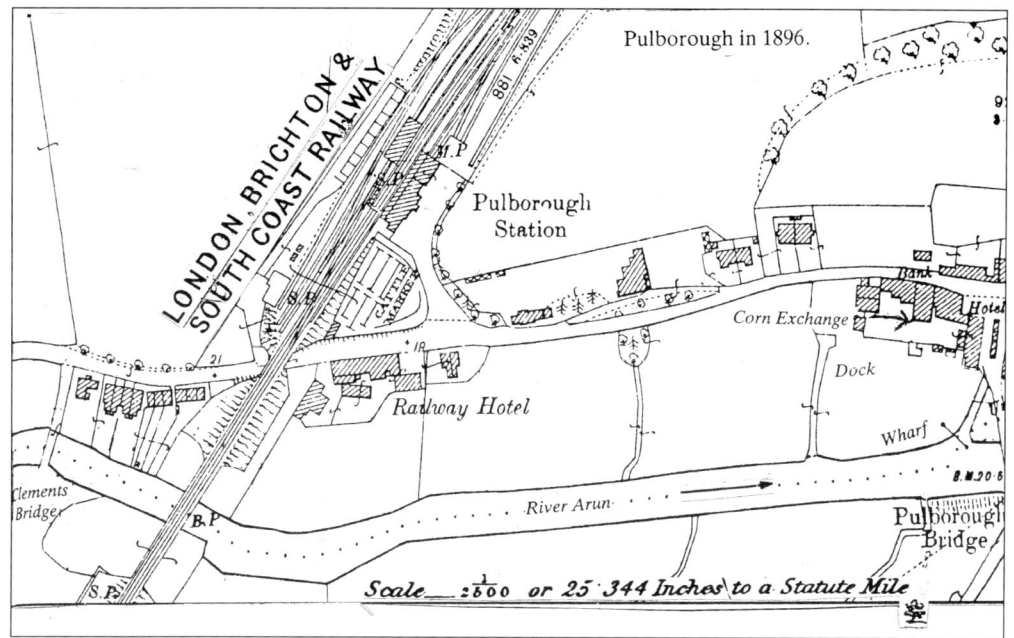

Pulborough in 1896.

A 1930s view shows the buildings adjoining the eighteenth century Swan Hotel which had been converted from stabling to garages. The first meeting of the proprietors of the Arun Navigation Company was held here on 6 June 1785.

Pulborough Wharf *c*.1920. The barge repair dock can be seen at left centre next to Float's hut, from which he let punts and skiffs. The building at left was the fishmonger's and greengrocer's shop of Harry Fielder, which stood in the middle of the highway until it was demolished in 1935. Pulborough Church stands in the background.

River traffic was often halted by floods for weeks at a time during the nineteenth century. Even today the causeway between Swan Bridge and Coldwaltham is sometimes flooded after heavy rain. Before the Second World War this was a regular occurrence which this 1937 photograph typifies. Beyond the 30mph warning sign is the ubiquitous circular AA yellow and black village sign of Pulborough, denoting its population, location and distance from London.

Clements Bridge, Pulborough. This drawing of the reed-infested river made by Thomas Evershed in 1843 indicates the difficulty barges had in using the river above Pulborough. The house was the local bobby's residence and the tower of Pulborough Church can be seen at top left.

Clements Bridge, viewed here in 1895, was built in around 1793. Its ostensible purpose was to provide access to the meadows for cattle; however, its low arches suggest that its main object was to discourage barges using the toll-free river instead of Hardham Tunnel.

Another view showing how dilapidated Clements Bridge had become by 1934.

Although token repairs were made from time to time, the bridge was eventually swept away by flood water in the early morning of 16 September 1968. The river authority removed the ruined piers and used the stone blocks to raise the river wall at Templemead.

Horses towing barges had to cross the river Arun at Stopham by this wooden 'gallows' bridge i.e. a flat beam high above the water with an inclined plane on each side. This 1889 view shows Hardham Mill in the background.

The wooden bridge seen here, c.1910, was replaced by a red iron structure in 1914.

Seven
The Coldwaltham Cut

The entrance to Coldwaltham Lock in 1941, more than fifty years after it had last been used to allow barges to circumnavigate the winding river to Stopham via Pulborough.

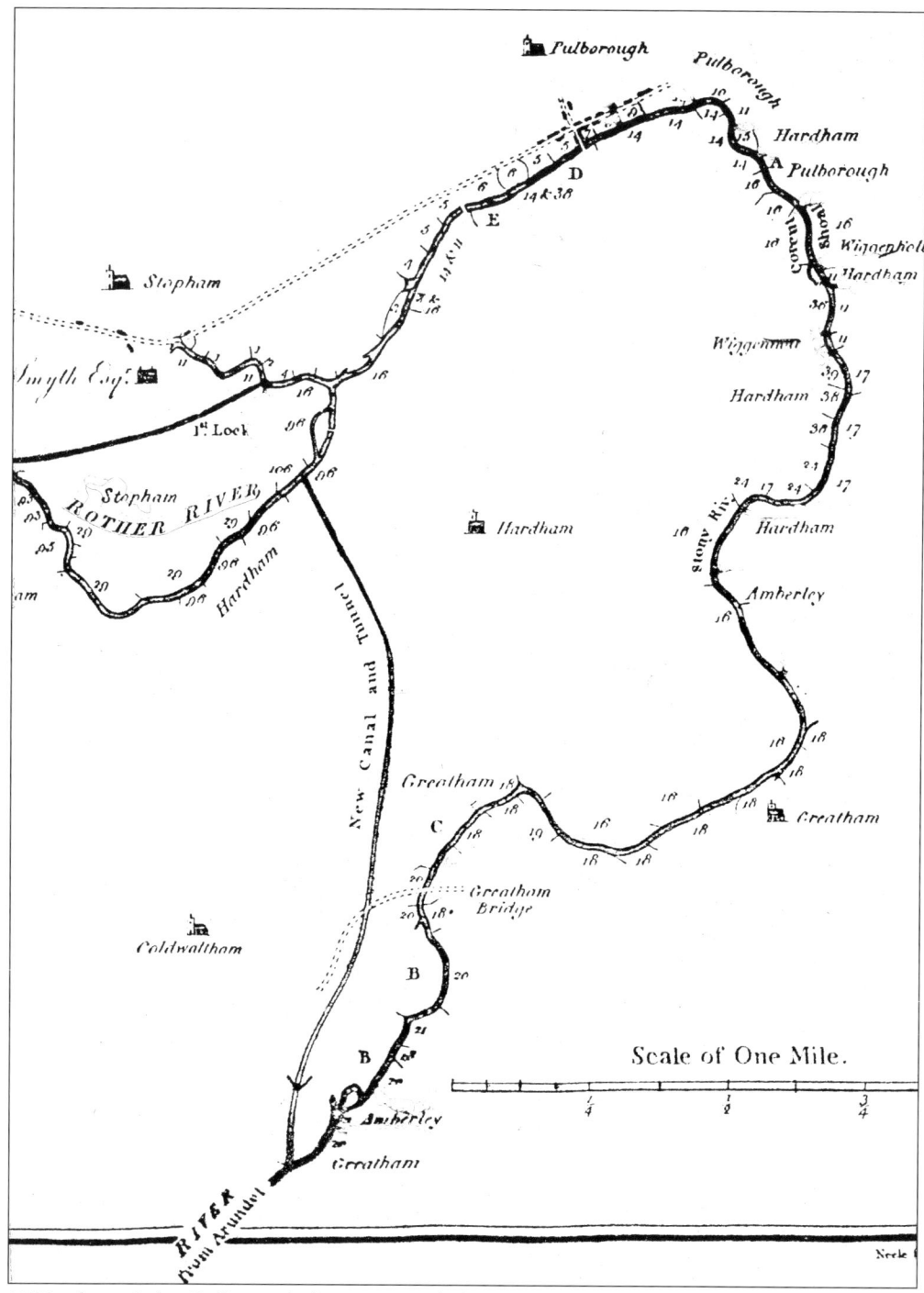

1793 plan of the Pulborough by-pass canal from Coldwaltham to Stopham via Hardham Tunnel. The new cut reduced the distance by 3¼ miles, but if barges came up with the tide only six hours were saved by using the tunnel. However the toll charge of 9 pence a ton, according to the Revd Arthur Young writing in the 1790s, drove traffic to 'its old channel' except when the river was too shallow or in flood.

The entrance to Coldwaltham Lock in 1908.

The entrance to Coldwaltham Lock at low-tide in 1933. The lock-house is in the background at right.

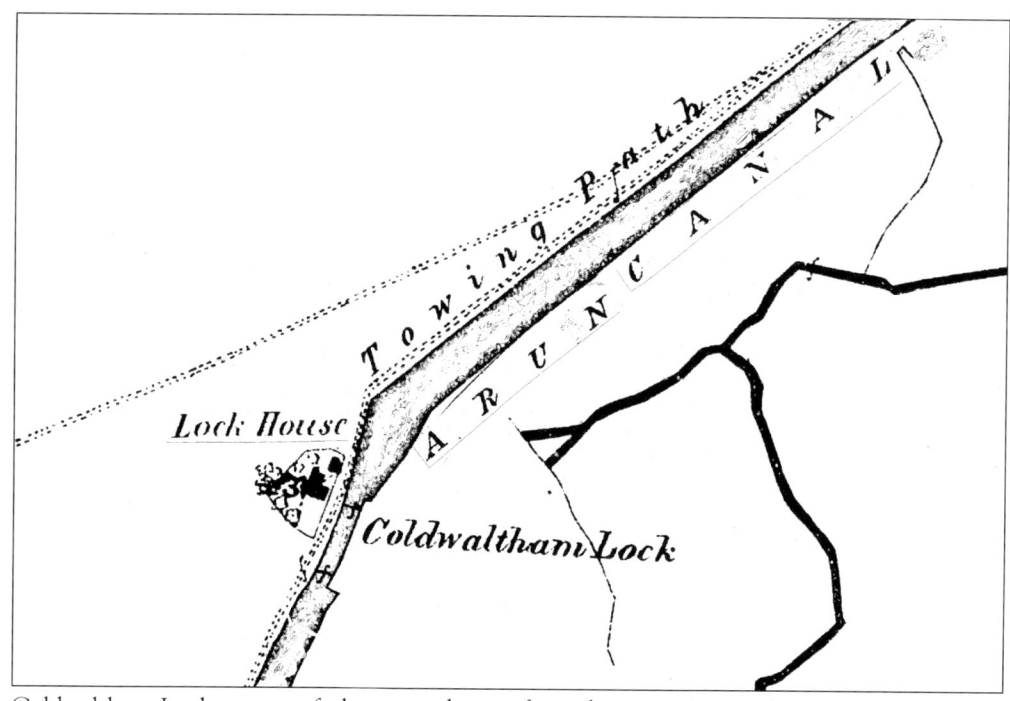

Coldwaltham Lock was two furlongs up the cut from the river Arun. This 1876 25 inch plan shows the lock-house and garden. Note also the winding hole immediately above the lock where barges moored while waiting for the tide to turn.

The roofless lock-house at Coldwaltham in 1908. The lock-keeper and his family must have had a difficult life since his home was flooded in most winters. One winter's day in the nineteenth century the old keeper fell into the lock and was drowned before the eyes of his helpless wife. Another lock-keeper was best known for always being 'toxacaped'.

Gradually over the years the walls of the old lock-house crumbled. Besides being regularly washed by floods, it was also used during the Second World War for local target practice by the Canadian Army. This view shows all that remained in 1950.

The southerly approach to the lock in 1950.

Looking toward the South Downs and Coldwaltham Lock in 1983.

Site of the canal bridge over the Coldwaltham to Greatham Road, 1950.

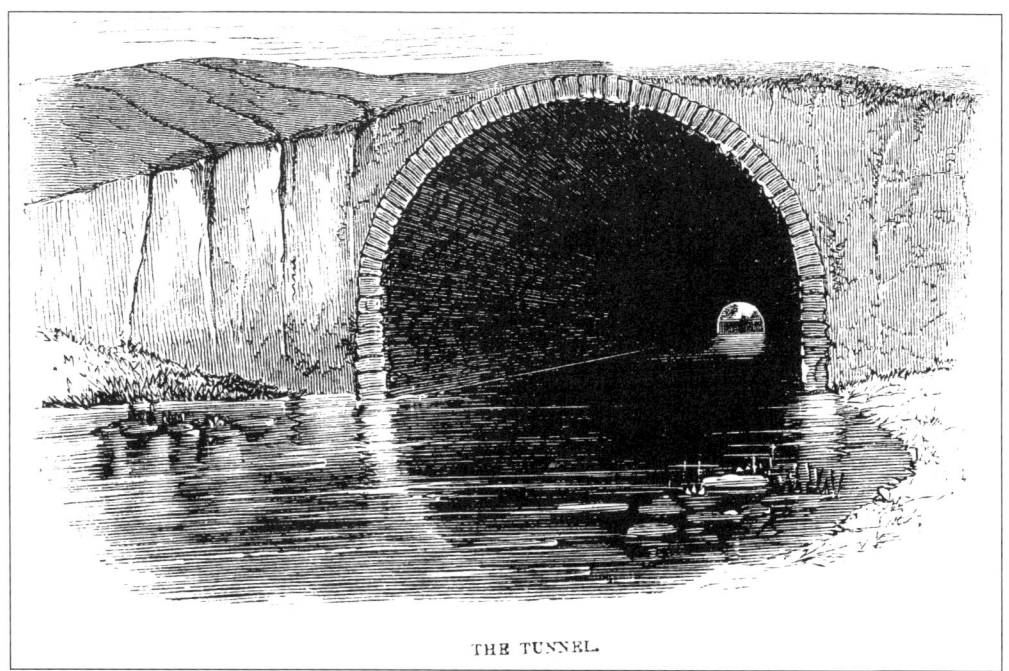

THE TUNNEL.

Artist's drawing in 1868 of the south entrance to Hardham Tunnel, showing Tunnel Lock at the far end. The tale is still told of how, in the 1880s, young Jim Strudwick was pushed out of the tunnel by other bargees travelling south, who in their haste to catch the ebbing tide at Coldwaltham refused quite correctly to give him the right of way.

The southern entrance as it appeared in 1949. Until the 1950s it was possible to paddle a rubber boat through as far as the earth bank raised beneath the main railway line to prevent subsidence in 1898. The author can report that the roof, floor and walls of the tunnel were all brick-lined. The water was some three feet deep and crystal clear. Stalactites hung from the roof but there were no bats, as are found in Greywell Tunnel on the Basingstoke Canal.

The north end of Hardham Tunnel, 1843. Observe the crude tree trunks used as beams for the lock gates. Dashwood passed through what he termed 'the chalk cliff' at Hardham by punting his boat along by means of pushing the boat-hook against the roof. 'In the middle it became quite dark and we could only just guide ourselves by means of the bright outlet at the end. The roof was covered in stalactites, and in places the water fell upon us from crevices above in heavy drops so that we had to try and steer clear of them where we heard their splashes on the water below. It took about ten minutes to pass through the subterranean passage...'

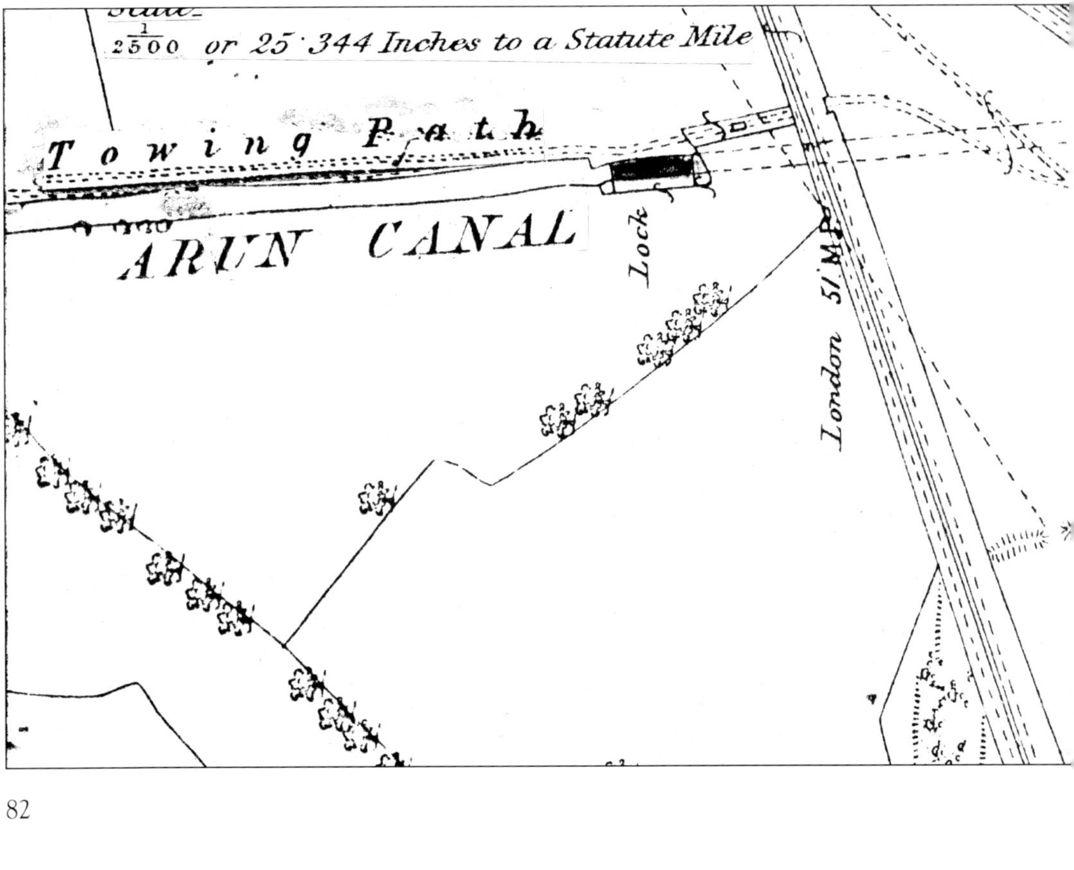

The remains of the upper gate to Tunnel Lock in 1951.

Below: The 1876 ordnance survey map shows how the tow-path was carried by a brick underpass beneath the railway track to Petworth which was built in 1859. When the railway was opened through the Arun valley to Ford the tow-path was carried over the line by an accommodation bridge. It was not an easy path to follow. In 1867 Dashwood was detained here some little while as the groom leading the pony had lost his way.

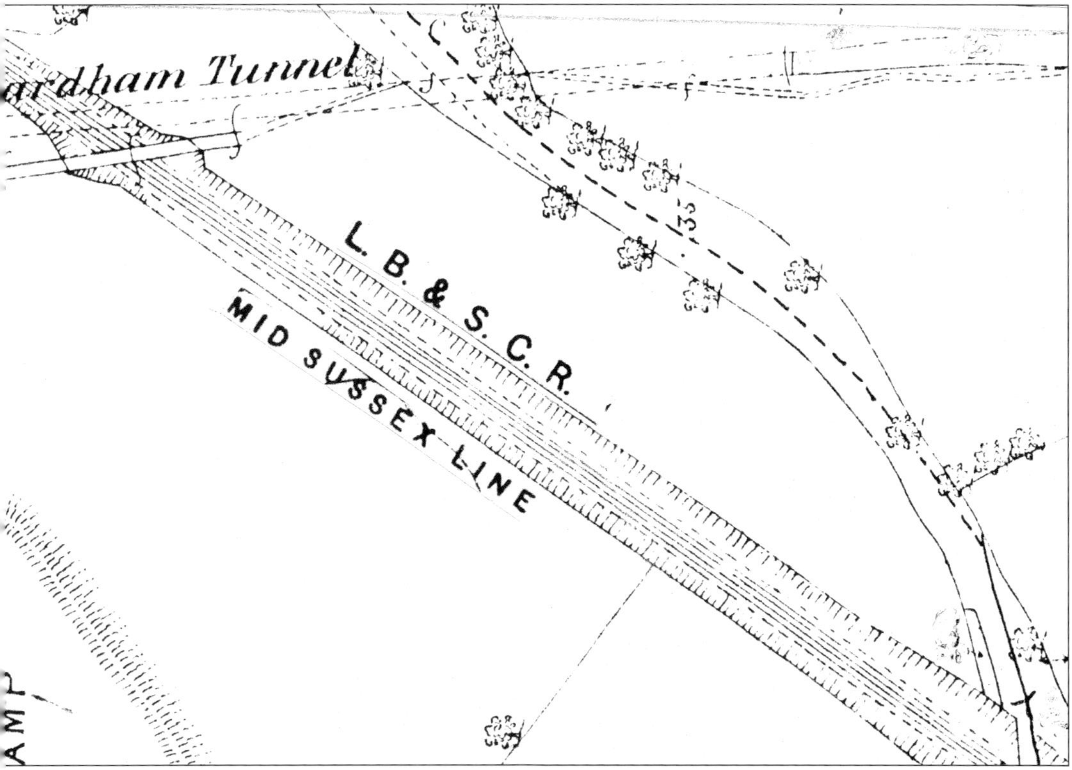

Hardham Tunnel – north entrance. The concrete dam was built by the water authority on the site of Tunnel Lock in 1952. Note the state of preservation of one of the lock beams which had formed part of one of the gates. The entrance to the brick underpass for horses which was built when the Pulborough-Petworth railway was opened in 1859 was to the left of the tunnel.

Canal tunnels there were in plenty, but Hardham Tunnel is unique in being the only one in Great Britain to have been used to avoid the bends of a river navigation. In Europe they are found on the Saône and other rivers. This close up view of the north entrance was taken in 1951.

The head of water penned by the building of Hardham Lock was later used to operate the corn mill built by George Sharp of Guildford in 1827. In this 1843 drawing the lock-cottage and lock-gates can be seen at right. The corn mill was bombed by the Germans in 1942 and subsequently demolished. The barge at left would probably have come up from Littlehampton to the mill via Pulborough to avoid payment of the tunnel toll of nine pence a ton.

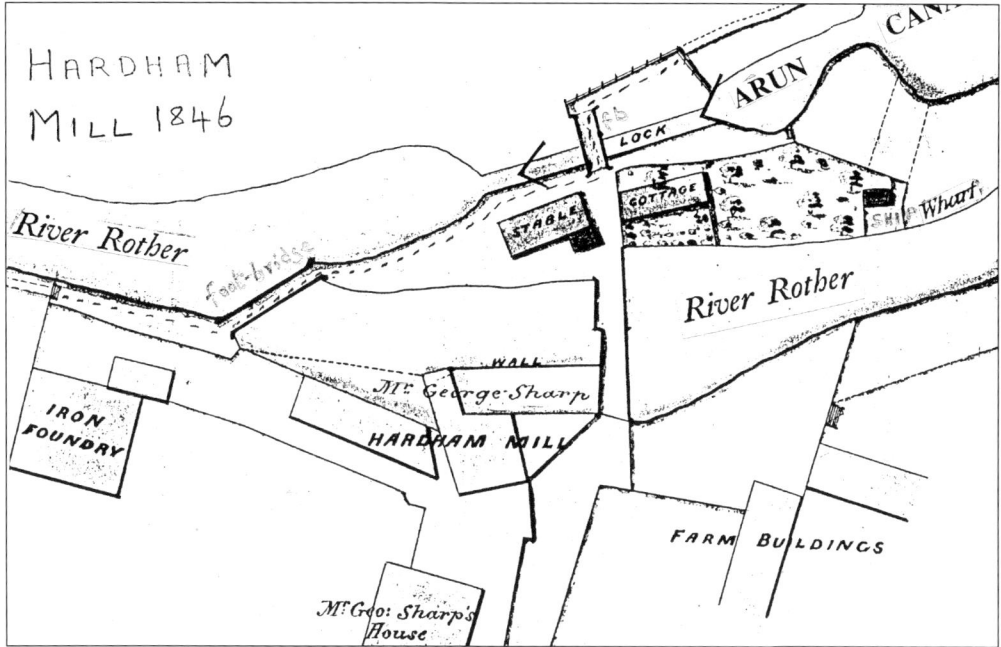

The corn mill was built after the Arun Navigation had been opened. The ninety-nine year lease dated 4 June 1827 granted George Sharp the right to use all the waste water running out of the river near Hardham Lock at 6d a year. It is surprising to find a footbridge (presumably swivel) lying across the centre of Hardham Lock. Its headroom is not known, but in July 1867 Dashwood's una boat nearly sank when its seven foot mast became wedged under the bridge as the lock was filled.

Hardham Lock, 1889. It was here that twenty-two years earlier Mrs Dashwood (of pleasure boating fame) nearly came to grief when Dashwood's una boat *Caprice* drifted under an iron footbridge which crossed the lock. Barges coming down from London passed beneath Stopham Bridge and near to the entrance to the Rother Navigation before entering the River Rother. The lock at Hardham Mill enabled barges bound for Portsmouth to enter the Arun Canal and pass through Hardham Tunnel. The toll was 9d a ton, but it saved the extra miles entailed in passing along the tidal river past Pulborough where shallows could be a problem at low water.

The entrance to Hardham Lock in 1941. The lock-keeper's cottage was demolished in 1956 and the lock filled in by the river authority in 1968.

Eight

The Rother Navigation

A line of poplars indicates the entrance to the Rother Navigation at Stopham in 1952. Turn right for Stopham Bridge and Pallingham. Eight locks enabled barges to cover the twelve miles to Midhurst. An account of the history of the navigation will be found in *London's Lost Route to Midhurst*(see bibliography).

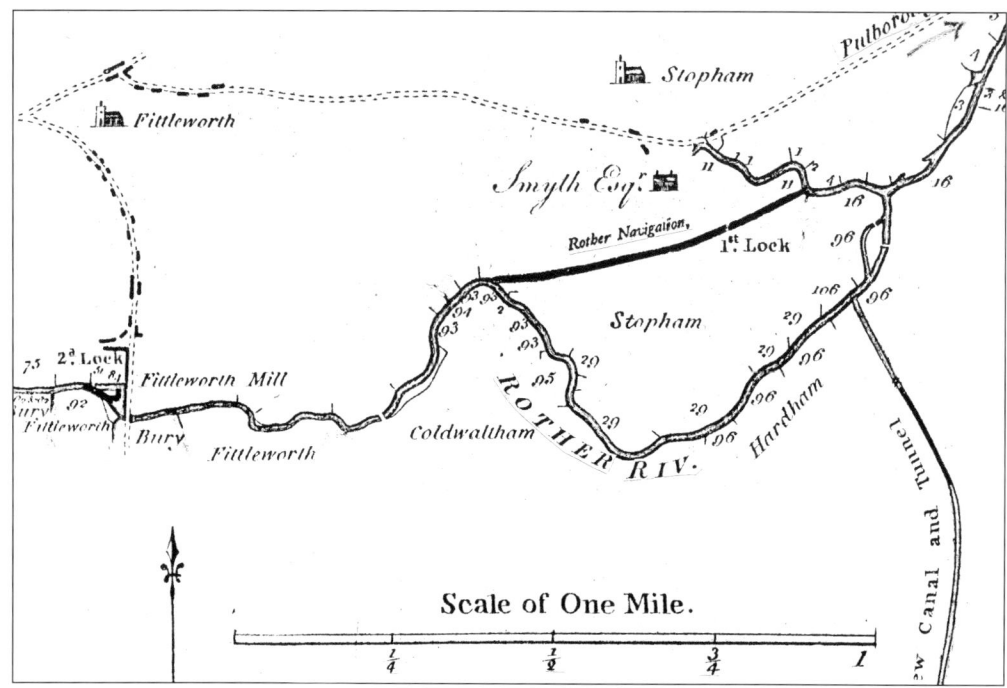

1793 plan showing the entrance to the Rother Navigation from the river Arun.

The author and his wife forcing a passage up the Rother Navigation from the junction with the Arun Navigation at Stopham to the first lock in August 1987. (Photo: Dieter Jebens).

The approach to the Arun Navigation from Stopham Lock can only be navigated nowadays at flood tides and even then only with difficulty.

The entrance to Stopham Lock chamber in 1987. Surprisingly little has altered since the navigation ceased to be used in 1888, although the remains of the lock gates have long since disappeared.

The stone occupation bridge which was built over the navigation in 1792 as it cut through the grounds of Stopham House. The bridge is still in everyday use for farm traffic.

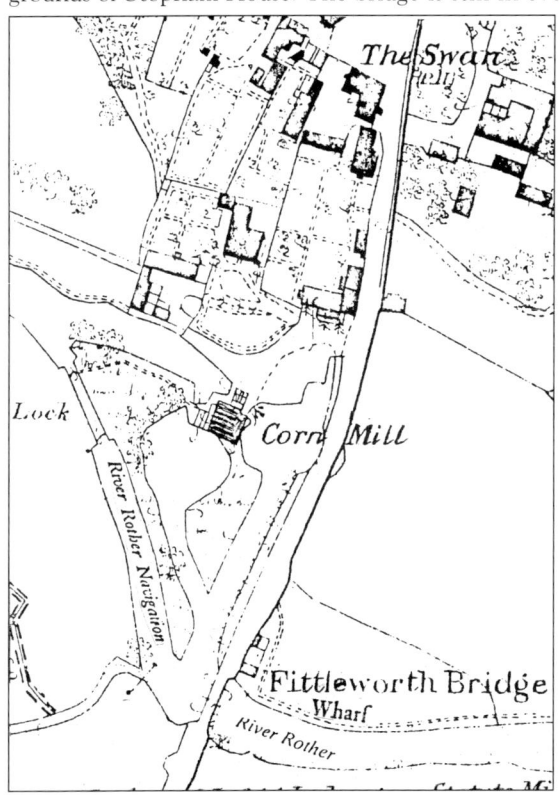

Map of Fittleworth in 1876 showing the location of the wharf and the lock.

90

This painting by Henry Moore shows a barge moored at Fittleworth Wharf in 1863. Observe the simple gang plank, the long pole and the bowler hats worn by the bargees.

A watercolour by A.W. Weedon showing a barge moored below Fittleworth Bridge in 1875.

No amount of pushing would have opened the lock-gates at Fittleworth when this photograph was taken in 1899, eleven years after the last barge had passed through.

Received 3^d *March* 18&3

ROTHER

Navigation Tolls.

A. Whitting, Collector
per Henry Upton

From 27 Dec 42 to 17 Feby 1843

£	s	d
96	17	9

Every month or so for over thirty years Anthony Whitting, the lock-keeper and collector of tolls at Fittleworth, sent a list of all traffic and money received to Lord Egremont's steward at Petworth House. After the navigation was closed Whitting ran the local grocery but in the national census of 1891 he is described as 'grocer retired'.

Fittleworth Mill is best known for the oil painting finished in 1835 by John Constable. However, a mill stood to the west of this building in the thirteenth century. In 1615 it was recorded that there was a malt mill and a wheat mill in one timber building, close to which was a rude wharf supported by timber.

This view was taken in around 1907 when pleasure boating was very popular. The mill continued to grind corn until the 1920s. It is now a private residence.

Pleasure skiffs passing through the remains of Shopham Lock in the summer of 1895.

ROTHER NAVIGATION.

No. *223*

Name of Owner : *Stoveld* Number : *13*
Kind of Lading : *Coals*
Quantity : *30* Tons, Cwts.
Whence brought : *From the Arun*
Where to be landed : *Rotherbridge*
Distance of Navigation : *5* Miles, *6* Furlongs.

	£	s	d
TONNAGE	2	3	1½
WHARFAGE	—	15	—
	2	18	1½

Toll Collector.

Bill of lading issued by the toll collector at Fittleworth to timber and coal merchant William Stoveld whose barge *No. 13* on this occasion carried 30 tons of coal from the Arun to Rotherbridge in July 1842. The average number of barges licensed annually to use the navigation was between fifty and sixty in the 1840s. Coal and chalk were the main cargoes upstream, timber downstream.

Coultershaw Flour Mill, c.1905. The mill was burnt down in 1923, later rebuilt in ferroconcrete and subsequently demolished. This view is taken from the coal wharf on the north bank. The entrance to the lock is left of the picture.

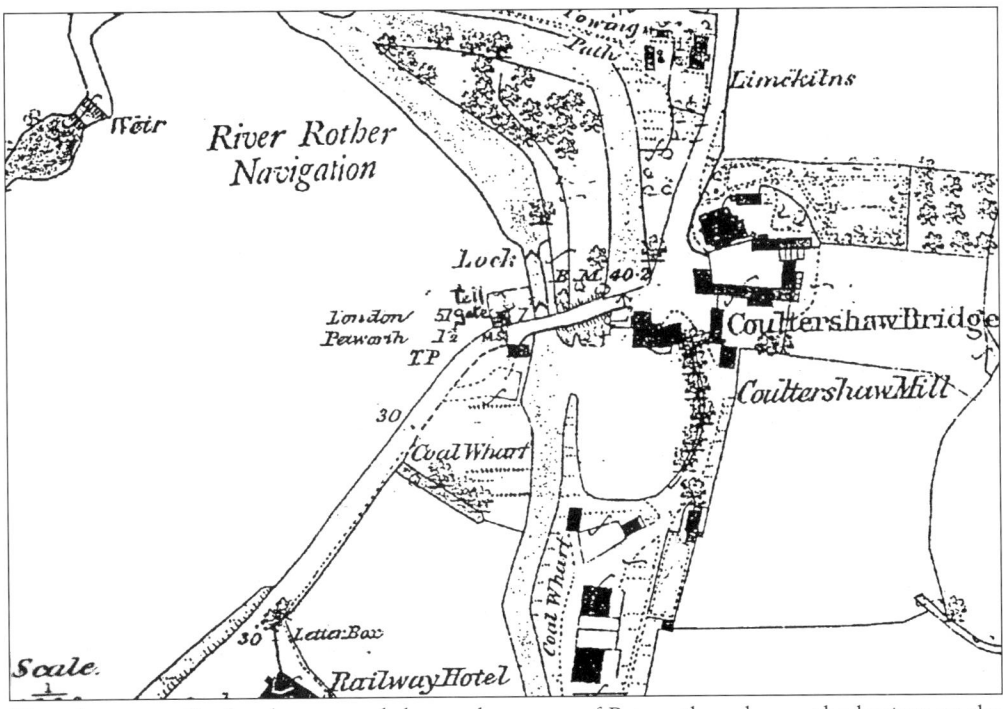

The wharves at Coultershaw served the market town of Petworth and were the busiest on the Rother Navigation. (1875 ordnance survey).

Miles		ROTHER.
	Iping Bridge	
2	Stedham Mill -	Portage.
4	Woolbeding Mill -	Portage.
6¾	Midhurst Mill -	Portage. For next mile and a half the route is through Cowdray Park.
7¼	Midhurst Wharf -	Under little bridge, right bank. Stats. L. & S. W. and L. B. & S. C. Rs. Hotel, Angel. Landlord can cart boat from station. Cowdray Park (Earl of Egmont) always open and Cowdray Ruins worth seeing.
9	Todham Lock -	Portage right bank. The lower gates having been removed the upper are converted into sluice gates.
10¼	Moorland Lock -	Lock-cut sharp to left just above the sluice. Entrance is sometimes choked with weeds and difficult to see. On no account go round by backwater, which is blocked by fallen trees and low bridge.
11	Lodge Bridge Lock	Lock-cut is narrow channel by left bank. The broader one on right leads to Selham, a pretty village (Stat. L. B. & S. C. R.) Look out for clay-reefs in channel below.
12¼	Lady Weir - -	Lower boat down wall side at right of sluice. Picturesque spot.
13¼	Kelsham Floating Bridge -	Chained to left bank. Easily moved (1894). Pretty reaches below.
14¾	Coultershaw Lock -	Stat. L. B. & S. C. R. (right bank). Lock-cut on the right blocked (1894). Go on straight to mill, take out on right bank, carry along road to the right and launch from meadow. Petworth village 1½ mile left bank. Petworth House (Earl of Egremont) has fine paintings, sculpture, &c.; open on Thursdays. George Lambell, carrier, Petworth, goes to Guildford every Friday, and will take canoe from Coultershaw Bridge to the Wey (p. 11) or vice versa for 5s.
15⅝	Shopham Lock -	Strong stream in lock-cut. Lock has no gates and water rushes through. Can be easily shot. Before doing so land and reconnoitre, as on a full river snags sometimes get jammed athwart entrance. From here to Fittleworth more open but still beautiful country.
18	Fittleworth Lock -	Stat. L. B. & S. C. R. Lock-cut blocked. Go on to mill and portage on left bank. Look out for stones below mill. Inn, Swan (good 1894). Great place for artists. See room with painted panels and "Visitors' Book." Miller can house boat.
19½	Stopham Lock	Lock-cut was (1894) blocked by felled trees—probably only temporarily. It is possible to go over little weir on right at entrance to cut and by backwater (1 mile) to Hardham Mill Lock, where is easy portage close to Arun. One mile down this backwater, on right, is the entrance to Arun Canal (disused) which led through Hardham Tunnel and Waltham Lock to Arun 2 miles above Amberley.
19⅝	River Arun Junc.	

Extract from the 1896 edition of the Oarsman's Guide about the Rother Navigation. The distances shown are from Iping Bridge. All the locks were unworkable but the condition of most of the lock chambers remains unchanged a century later.

The Rother Navigation Act allowed Lord Egremont to build a branch canal from Shopham to Haslingbourne Bridge near Petworth. This was opened in 1795 and was intended to be extended to join the Wey Navigation at Shalford, but in the event Lord Egremont decided to promote an easier route using the Wey & Arun Junction Canal, opened in 1816. The Petworth Canal was closed in 1826 and the two locks dismantled. The bed was partially infilled but is discernible after heavy rain as this 1963 photograph reveals.

The lock chamber at Moorland Lock in 1982. The Oarsman's Guide stated that on no account should one go round by the backwater which is blocked by fallen trees, but the authoress Eleanor Barnes nearly drowned here while canoeing down the Rother before the First World War.

Rotherbridge Farmhouse and the site of Rotherbridge, pulled down in 1801. The bridge was replaced in the 1890s by Kelsham Floating Bridge, a curious structure used as a footbridge which, Bonthron noted on his trip down the Rother, could be opened by raising one end. This view was taken in around 1925 and the bridge was replaced by a fixed suspension bridge in 1935 and by an iron bridge with tubular railings in 1961.

The new wooden footbridge at Rotherbridge in 1935.

The canal basin at Midhurst viewed *c.*1898, was the terminus of the Rother Navigation. The tow-path passed beneath the bridge, built in 1794, which was restored as part of the town's commemoration of Queen Elizabeth's Silver Jubilee in 1977.

After the navigation ceased to be used for barge traffic, skiffs were available for hire at the wharf. This ceased in 1912 when Mr. Port's boat-house was destroyed by fire. The Midhurst gasometer can be seen at right.

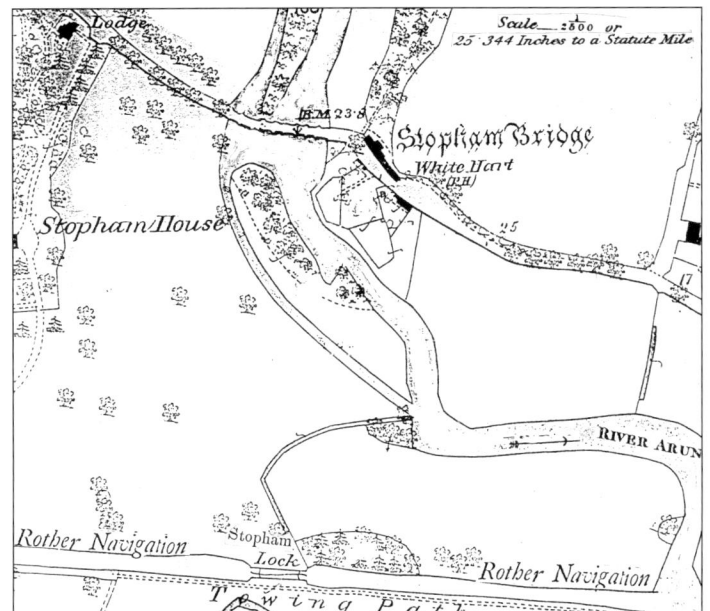

Ordnance 25 inch survey, 1876, showing the junction of the Arun and Rother Navigations at Stopham.

The boat-house at Stopham House in around 1950. It was built soon after the turn of the century and was much used at the time of the local regatta. Only its foundations remained after the great flood of 1968 when the high wall beside the main road was also swept away.

Nine
Stopham Bridge to Pallingham

The White Hart at Stopham Bridge, 1952. The bridge was built during the reign of Edward III. In the seventeenth century a drawbridge facilitated the passage of boats. In 1822 the central arch was raised to allow more heavily laden barges to pass.

Before the First World War and until about 1924 the reach above Stopham Bridge was the setting of the annual regatta, seen here taking place in 1912.

Stopham Wharf in around 1875. The central navigation arch is to the right and the bridge's remaining arches are hidden by trees. Even so the bridge's elevation appears distorted and there are in fact three not two arches to the left of the central arch. Artistic licence in the extreme.

Sam Strudwick's partner, Loyd Saigeman, on the *Reliance* above Stopham Bridge in 1905.

The Strudwick family were well known on the Rother and Arun Navigations. William (1815-1888) had been master of the *Albion* and had carried many cargoes of hoops and timber down the Rother. His brother John (1821-1903) bequeathed his furniture and one cow to his widow and the remainder of his livestock, his house and his ageing barge *Eleanor* to his son Sam (1864-1933). In 1905 *Eleanor* was replaced by the *Reliance* and used primarily for the brick traffic from Harwoods Green down to Arundel and for carrying sand from Littlehampton, coal and culm from Arundel and chalk from Houghton up to Pulborough and Stopham. In 1923 *Reliance* was sold to the Arun Brick Company of Rackham. Here the *Reliance* is shown moored above Stopham Bridge in 1905.

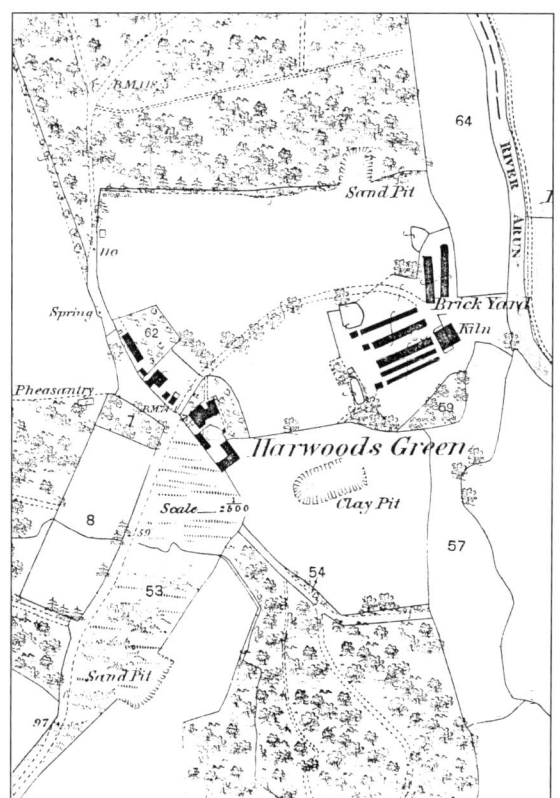

Map of the brickyard at Harwoods Green, Stopham as it was in 1876. It was established in the eighteenth century. Most of its output was moved by water both upstream and down. The yard continued in regular use until about 1905 and was not finally abandoned until 1922.

The entrance to the Arun Canal at Pallingham as viewed in 1952. The $4\frac{1}{2}$ mile waterway to Newbridge, Wisborough Green was in use from 1787 until 1888. It was operated independently of the Wey & Arun Canal and remained open for seventeen years after the junction canal had closed.

Ten
The Arun Canal to Newbridge

Pallingham Double Lock – fully laden barges often had insufficient water to enter Pallingham Lock so, before the opening of the Portsmouth & Arundel Canal, it was agreed to increase the draught. A lower lock was constructed in 1822 which increased the depth of water over the cill by 18 inches. The remains of the lower gate posts can be seen in this 1934 photograph.

The entrance to Pallingham Lock was photographed in about 1918. The lock cottage was from 1792 always occupied by a member of the Stone family. James Stone was lock-keeper for thirty-nine years and his son Benjamin Stone, who had been appointed lock-keeper in 1871, lived there until his death on 31 August 1935. The mooring posts are clearly visible as well as the pleasure boat used by Ben Stone, who is seen wearing his black hat.

Pallingham Lock was one of the deepest locks between Littlehampton and Weybridge, having a rise and fall of 7 to 9 feet dependent on the amount of water coming down the river and the tide. It could admit barges up to 68ft 3in, with a beam of 11ft 9in. This view was taken in 1952.

Benjamin Stone, who was lock-keeper from 1871 to 1888, seen standing by the footbridge over the lock. As a boy Stone had been a shepherd on the hills and after the closing of the canal had done a fair amount of carpentry, including making shepherds' stools. Thurston Hopkins described these home-made contrivances as being 'rather in the nature of an up-to-date cane and nickel-plated shooting stick'.

In the matter of the Companies Act, 1862,

In the matter of the Company of the Proprietors of the Wey and Arun Junction Canal.

BY AN ORDER made by his Honor the Vice Chancellor, SIR RICHARD MALINS, in Chambers in the above matter, dated the 26th day of May, 1871, on the application of the Official Liquidator of the above named Company, it was ordered as follows : "It is ordered that Notice be inserted in the *London Gazette*, the *Times Newspaper*, the *West Sussex Gazette*, the *Surrey Standard* Newspaper, and the *Surrey Advertiser* Newspaper ; and by Bills posted in the Towns of *Arundel* and *Guildford*, and along the Route of the said Canal, that an application has been made to the Court for the closing for traffic of the said Canal (extending from Stonebridge in the Parish of Shalford, in the County of Surrey, to Newbridge in the Parish of Wisborough Green, in the County of Sussex, the property of the above named Company), and the extinguishment of all rights of way, or user, and other rights in reference thereto, or in connection therewith, on or after the 1st day of July next: And that such application will be further heard and considered on the 24th day of June next, at the Chambers of the said Judge, No. 3, Stone Buildings, Lincolns Inn, in the County of Middlesex, at 12 of the Clock

Above: Pallingham Lock voucher

Pallingham Lock House, where tolls were collected by five members of the Stone family from the time of the opening of the Arun Canal until its closure in 1888. The house contained in 1911 a living room with cupboard, kitchen, scullery with fireplace, bakery and grocer's shop. Upstairs were three tiny bedrooms, one with fireplace. On the adjacent wharf were located boarded and brick, pantiled and slated store rooms, a privy, a fowl house and a small stable. This view taken in 1952 shows the lock-keeper's old skiff leaning against the wall. The extensions at each end of the house were remodelled in the late 1930s.

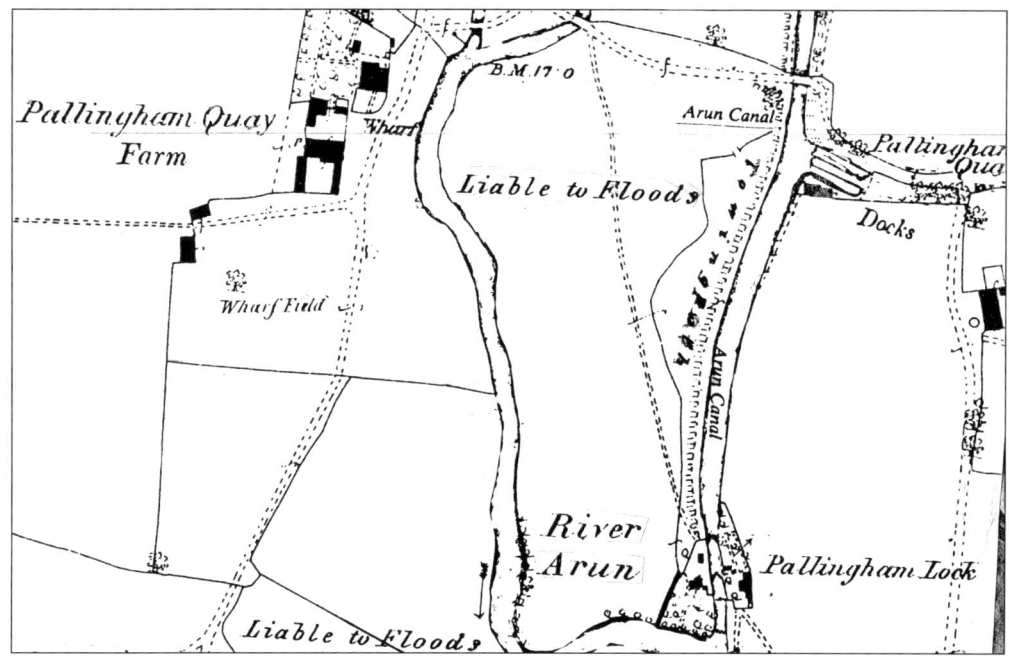

Pallingham Lock, Docks and Quay – the 1875 ordnance survey shows the lock which had been completed in 1787 and the barge building and repair yard which was opened in 1804. The building marked south of the two docks was the carpenter's shop built of timber and thatch. The quay on the river Arun had been used since the reign of Queen Elizabeth I for conveying timber by barge down to Arundel.

Pallingham Quay Farm from a drawing by Thomas Evershed in 1843. The 'wharf field' shown on eighteenth-century plans was to the left of the farm buildings beyond the river which was in the middle ground beyond the horses. The farmhouse, where Evershed was born, is partly shrouded by trees.

The entrance to Pallingham Docks and the barge building yard in 1952. It is a brave man who attempts to penetrate the all-embracing thicket which now covers the area and which remains in private ownership.

The Carpenter's Shop (1886) built of timber and thatch, where Benjamin Stone used to work. The docks were situated between the tree trunks and the two huts, in this southward view.

Above: Most of the brick and stone accommodation bridges ceased to be used after the canal bed ran dry and were left to slowly decay until the 1960s. Toat Farm Bridge was one of those rebuilt by the Wey & Arun Canal Trust with the help of the local landowner in 1985.

John Stepney, who lived on the banks of the Arun Canal at Haybarn on the Lee Place Estate, told the author that he was the last man to work a barge up from Pulborough to Newbridge Wharf, where its timbers were broken up and burnt in 1888. This photograph was taken in 1952 when John was eighty-six years of age.

Lee Farm (or Middle) Lock was one of three locks built on the Arun Canal in 1787. Each had single upper gates and double lower gates. This view was taken in September 1952.

A Wey & Arun Canal Trust voluntary working party rebuilding the west wall of Lee Farm Lock in May 1992. The trust hopes to reopen the Arun Canal from Newbridge to Pallingham after restoring the Wey & Arun Canal from Loxwood to Newbridge.

An 1896 picture of the brick and stone accommodation bridge built in 1787 below the turf-sided flood lock at Lording's (Orfold), Wisborough Green. (Francis Frith photograph courtesy of Worthing Central Library).

Culvert beneath the Arun Canal below Lording's Lock, 1957.

Lording's Flood Lock – the site of the brick and stone former accommodation bridge and lower gates of what were described in the 1821 Act of Parliament as a 'second pair of flood gates at Harford (sic) to form a one foot lock'. This was the only turf-sided lock on the navigation. The work of excavating the site at Orfold was carried out by Winston Harwood and his team of volunteers in 1994.

The remains of the lower gate of the flood lock in 1952. The lock was built in 1823 to help heavily laden barges to enter Lording's Lock. This was part of the improvement required to meet the expected increase of traffic upon the opening of the Portsmouth & Arundel Canal.

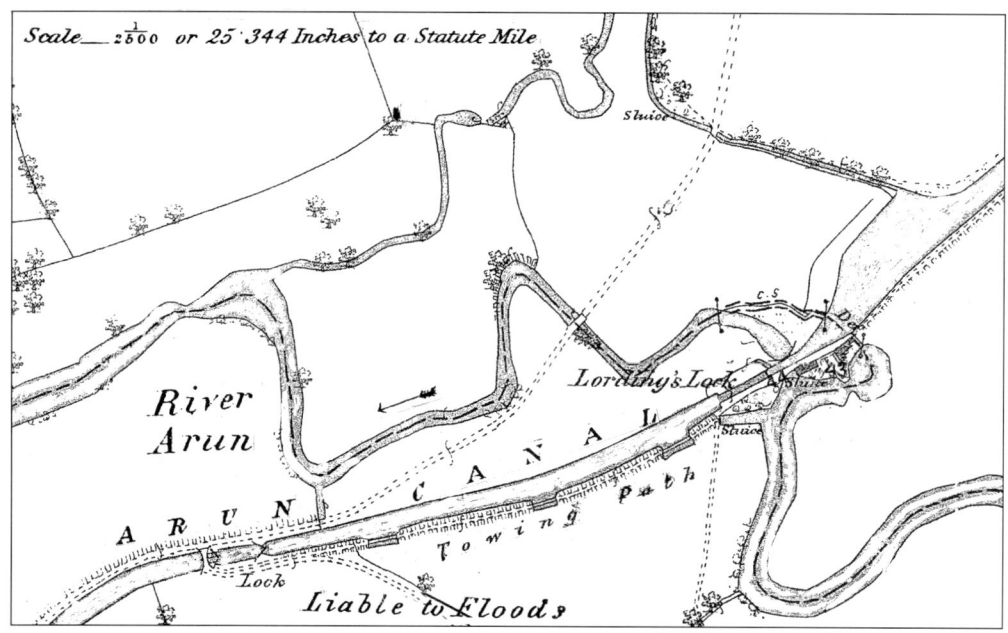

Scale — 1/2500 or 25·344 Inches to a Statute Mile

River Arun

Lording's Lock

ARUN CANAL

Towing Path

Lock

Liable to Floods

The 1876 survey shows the tributary stream to the Arun and the feeder stream coming down from Wisborough Green which supplied water to the top of the Arun Canal. Also marked is the turf-sided lock with the one foot rise.

Recent excavations have revealed part of the ground floor of the lock cottage by Lording's Lock. It was here that J.B. Dashwood watched the lock-keeper's wife and two pretty daughters making butter early one July morning in 1867.

To maintain the water level above Lording's Lock a water wheel was installed by the lock cottage. Its site and the water inlet can be seen in this 1990 photograph.

Lording's Lock and Orfold Aqueduct – the weir controlling the flow of water through the culverts under the aqueduct. The water wheel chamber can be seen to the right of the weir paddles in this 1957 photograph.

The lower section of Lording's Lock beyond the aqueduct, looking toward the flood lock in 1957. It was this area that was most subject to severe flooding and breached embankments, and as a result barge traffic between London and Portsmouth in the 1820s and 1830s was often held up for weeks at a time.

Cattle congregating below Lording's Lock in 1957. The canal bank, breached by floods, is visible in the background.

Orfold aqueduct carried the canal over the river Arun. By 1957 the west wall of the aqueduct had collapsed, but the east wall and culverts had been rebuilt and the paddle gear replaced to control the river's flow. The second view taken thirty years later shows little change.

ARUN NAVIGATION.

NEWBRIDGE WHARF.

NOTICE
IS HEREBY GIVEN, THAT
ON AND AFTER THE 1st OF APRIL, 1874,
THE
ARUN NAVIGATION PROPRIETORS

Will cease to be Wharfingers or receive or deliver Goods at NEWBRIDGE WHARF, in the Parish of Wisbro' Green, or be answerable for any Goods deposited there; the Wharf may, however, still be used at the risk of the Persons using the same.

Dated this 1st day of December, 1873,

(BY ORDER)

EDWARD ARNOLD,
CLERK TO THE PROPRIETORS.

PULLINGER, PRINTER, NORTH STREET, CHICHESTER.

Newbridge Wharf. After the closing of the junction canal in 1871 the Arun Navigation suffered an inevitable diminution of traffic. Toll receipts had fallen by more than three quarters from £1,066 in 1864 to only £255 in 1873, representing a drop in tonnage of nearly two thirds. The company's decision to cease being wharfingers was therefore an inevitable economy.

Guildenhurst Farm, Wisborough Green – the bed of the canal looking south from the site of the former accommodation bridge at Guildenhurst as it appeared in 1952.

In August 1823, William Cobbett passed by Newbridge on one of his 'rural rides' and noted its air of activity. 'At this there are large timber and coal yards, and kilns for lime. This appears to be a grand receiving and distributing place'. This view was taken in 1952.

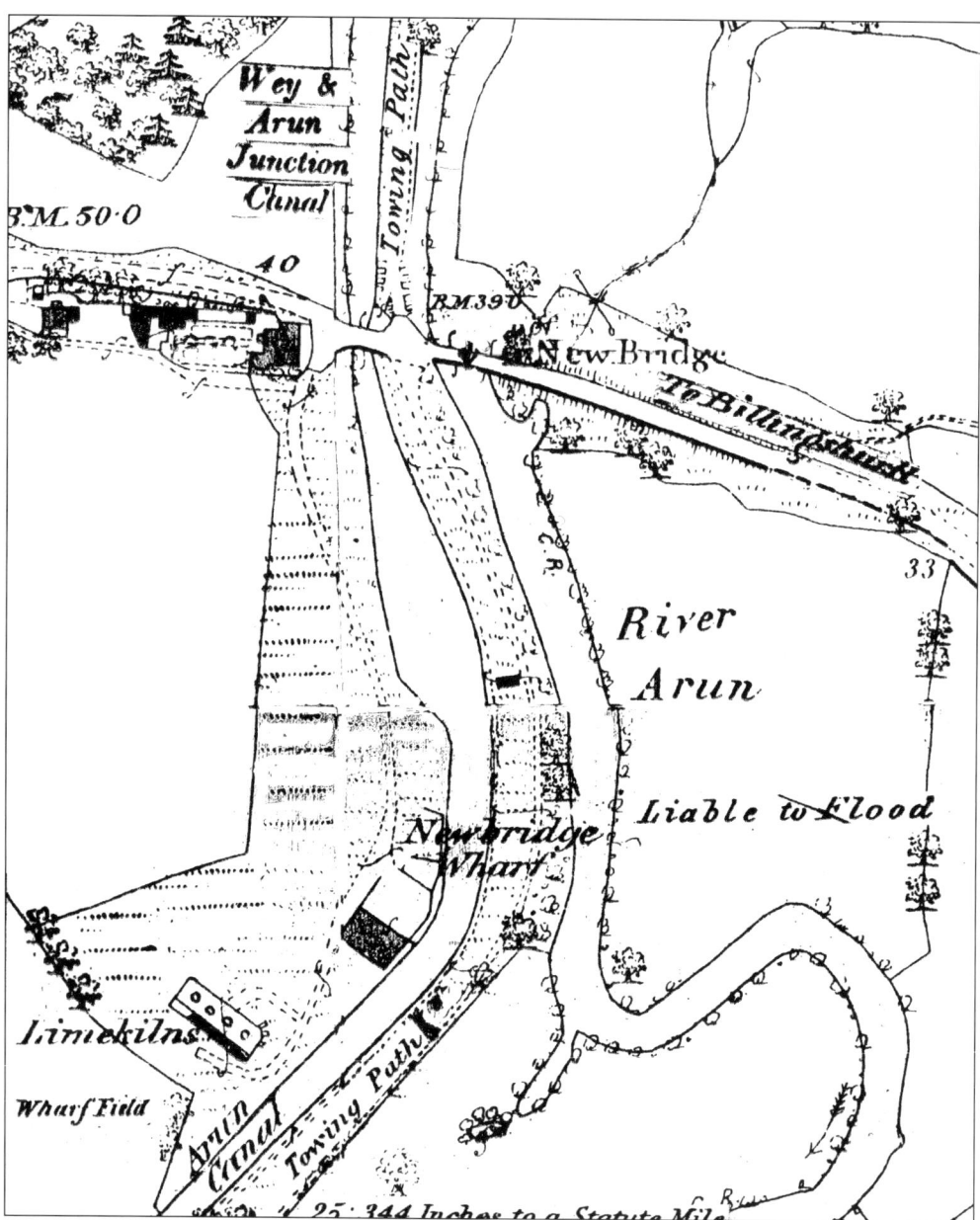

The former wharfinger's house at Newbridge, located on the 1876 ordnance survey beneath the figure 40, was situated at the entrance to Newbridge Wharf. In 1842 the house was owned by the Arun Navigation Company and occupied by Richard Seward, who was both the canal's superintendent and wharfinger (1828-1856), and was listed as the occupier of the beer shop and garden. By 1878 Thomas Stringer had become a beer retailer but by 1887 one of the buildings was listed as a shop.

The warehouse was built in 1839 when barge traffic was at its busiest. After the closure of the canal, it was used as a farm store (seen here in 1963) until purchased by Mr David Mitchell. It has now been converted into a luxury guest house.

Fred (standing on the bank) and Walter Dunkerton below Newbridge c.1885. Their father George Dunkerton was wharfinger from 1868 to 1886, by which time there was so little traffic that the arrangement was discontinued. The canal was closed in 1888 and sometime in the 1890s the family moved to Wheelers Farm in Wisborough Green where they began a dairy business.

Following page: An oil painting, probably painted shortly after the Wey & Arun Junction canal had been closed, showing the wharfinger's house at left and the canal bridge at Newbridge at centre. The position of the barges lying athwart the canal and the water lilies growing in profusion suggest a date around 1875.

The former wharfinger's house at Newbridge, Wisborough Green. During the period when Newbridge Wharf was, as William Cobbett described it, 'a grand receiving and distributing place', the wharfinger kept a beer house known locally as the Limeburners. After the navigation was closed, this reverted to a private dwelling.

Floods and lack of water were the main causes of traffic stoppages on the Arun Navigation, but the difficulties of trading were also worsened when the canal was frozen over. In January 1871 attempts by two bargees to break the ice with heavy hammers proved impossible and as recently as January 1963 it was possible for the author to walk across the ice below the bridge over the river at Newbridge. The river Arun was in fact covered from bank to bank as far as Pulborough.

ARUN NAVIGATION.

NOTICE.

The Navigation will be

CLOSED

on and from the 1st day of January, 1888, the Traffic being insufficient to meet the working expenses.

BY ORDER,

EDWARD ARNOLD,

CLERK.

Chichester.

13th December, 1887.

Notice of closure of the Arun Canal. After the closing of the Wey & Arun Junction Canal, traffic on the Arun Canal continued to decline in spite of the company making every effort to keep the navigation open. In 1882 forty-five ash and oak trees at Newbridge and Middle Lock were sold for £52; in 1883 the proprietors voluntarily contributed a similar sum to augment the dwindling receipts; the toll on coal was reduced to 3d a ton in 1885. Although no material revival of trade was expected, it was urged that keeping the canal open was in the public interest as it tended to keep down the railway rates. However, revenue continued to decline so the proprietors ordered the notice of closure to be posted along the tow-path in December 1887.

Newbridge, Wisborough Green, was the terminal point of the Wey & Arun Junction Canal. The canal bridge constructed in 1815 carried the turnpike road from Guildford to Pulborough and Arundel as well as being the main highway between Billingshurst, Wisborough Green and Petworth. This photograph was taken in 1954 after the bridge had undergone emergency support to carry the heavy traffic on the A272.

Railway and Canal Traffic Act, 1888.

River Arun Navigation.

APPLICATION FOR ABANDONMENT OF THE NAVIGATION.

Whereas The Company of Proprietors of the River Arun Navigation have applied to the Board of Trade, pursuant to section 45, sub-section 1, of the above Act, that the said Board of Trade should by Warrant signed by their Secretary authorise the abandonment of the Navigation belonging to the said Company, known as the River Arun Navigation, and the Canal forming part of such Navigation, by the existing Proprietors of the same, on the ground that the said Navigation and Canal are unnecessary for the purposes of Public Navigation within the meaning of the said section, and should make an order releasing the said Company or other the Proprietors of the Navigation and Canal from all liability to maintain the Navigation and Canal and from all statutory and other obligations in respect thereof or of or consequent on the abandonment thereof.

And Whereas the Board of Trade have directed Inquiry to be held by an Assistant Secretary of the Board of Trade into the subject matter of the said application for abandonment and to determine the amount of compensation (if any) to be paid to all persons entitled to compensation by reason of the proposed abandonment.

Notice is hereby given, that FRANCIS JOHN STEPHENS HOPWOOD, Esquire, C.M.G., the Assistant Secretary of the Board of Trade appointed to hold the said Inquiry, will attend for that purpose at the Norfolk Arms Hotel, Arundel, on Wednesday, the Fifteenth day of November, one thousand eight hundred and ninety-three, at eleven o'clock in the forenoon, and will then and there be prepared to hear and to receive the evidence of any person interested in the matter of the said Inquiry.

Dated this   day of one thousand eight hundred and ninety-three.

EDWARD ARNOLD,

Chichester.   **CLERK.**

ADCOCK, PRINTER, CHICHESTER.

Notice of Application for Abandonment, 1893. Although the Arun Canal had ceased to operate, it could not be abandoned until the Board of Trade had issued a warrant. Before it could do this a public enquiry had to be held, and when it took place in Arundel there were nine objections to the winding-up order. Not until September 1896 was the warrant obtained.

Acknowledgements

I should like to thank Martin Hayes of the West Sussex County Library Service, Ron Iden of the County Record Office and Susan White of Pulborough Library for their assistance in completing this work. I am particularly grateful to Dendy Easton, Dieter Jebens, J. Hayward Madden, David Mitchell, David Morris, Fred Saigeman and John Wood for the loan of illustrations. Peter Boyce helped with voyages of discovery and both Kay Bowen and Edwina Vine helped with the selection of plates and the typing of the manuscript.

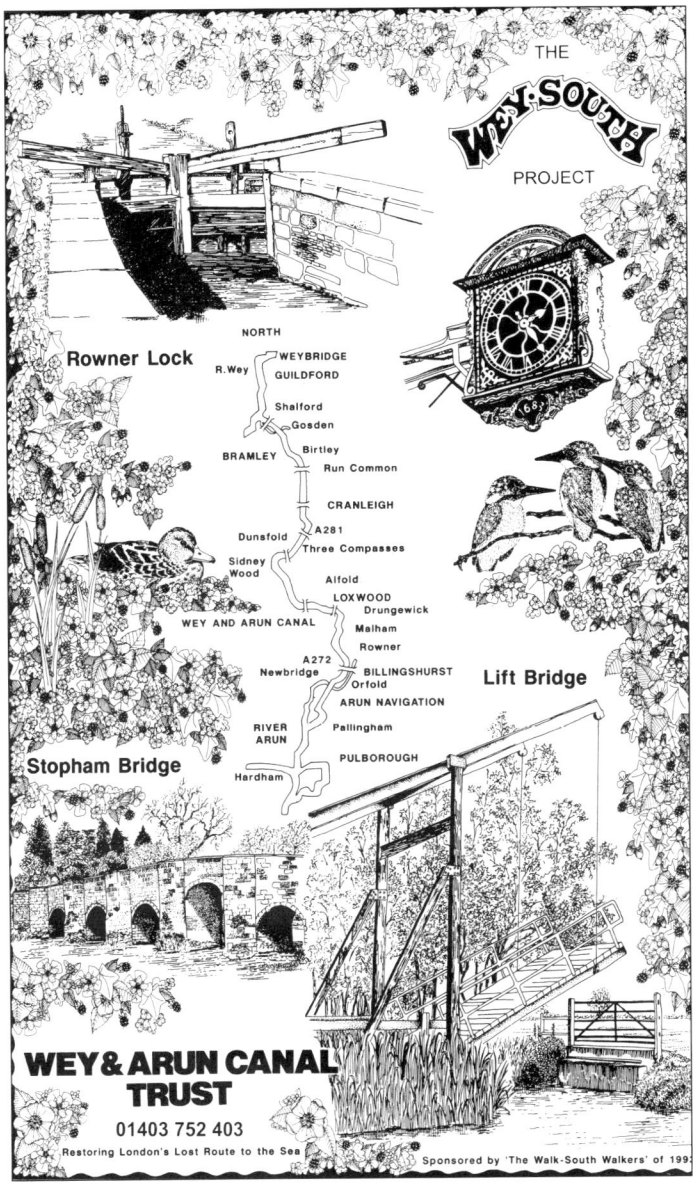

Bibliography

Dashwood, J.B. (1868) *The Thames to the Solent by Canal and Sea*
Allcroft, Hadrian A. (1930) *Waters of Arun*
Sellman, Roger (SCM 1935) *The Waterways of Sussex*
Goodsall, R.H. (1962) *The Arun and Western Rother*
Hadfield, Charles (1969) *The Canals of South and South-East England*
Thompson, H.J.F. (1974) *Littlehampton Long Ago*
Vine, P.A.L. (1996, 5th ed.) *London's Lost Route to the Sea*

Other works by P.A.L. Vine

London's Lost Route to the Sea (1965)
London's Lost Route to Basingstoke (1968)
The Royal Military Canal (1972)
Magdala (1973)
Ethiopia (1974)
Introduction to Our Canal Population: George Smith (1974)
Pleasure Boating in the Victorian Era (1983)
West Sussex Waterways (1985)
Surrey Waterways (1987)
Kent & East Sussex Waterways (1989)
Hampshire Waterways (1990)
London to Portsmouth Waterway (1994)
London's Lost Route to Basingstoke (1994, new ed.)
London's Lost Route to Midhurst (1995)
London's Lost Route to Portsmouth (in preparation)

The Wey & Arun Junction Canal (1999) Published by Tempus.